Black Belt: The '

Convento

PRAISE FOR BLACK BELT: THE WINNING EDGE!

"I am a big fan of Sal Convento and his belief that martial arts can help you achieve greater success in life. Read *Black Belt: The Winning Edge!* and let Sal's thinking impact the quality of your life."

Ken Blanchard
Coauthor, The One Minute Manager® and Leading at a Higher Level

"This powerful, practical book teaches you how thinking and acting like a Martial Artist actually shapes and develops your character and personality."

Brian Tracy
Author, The Power of Self-Confidence

"Sal Convento has written a book on a subject that every public school teacher wishes they could teach in their classroom. Sal has written a syllabus that should be mandatory to graduate. There is no standardized test to measure good character. However, this is the resume of skills that every employer wishes to hire. These are the values we want every family, friend and coworker to portray. I only wish the years I taught in the public school system I could have had more time to teach these skills to the students in my classroom. I believe we could prevent some of the suicides, bullying, and the mass shootings if we could teach these values in our school systems to every child. I look forward to the day when every child has "The Winning Edge!"

Teri Lee
President of Sunnyvale Martial Arts Academy
7th Degree Master Instructor

"Sal Convento, a martial arts warrior, takes the reader on a personal journey, expressing 13 Character Building principles and how they can impact your life. This book can serve as an inspiration to all who "Fight the Enemies Within." As you read *Black Belt: The Winning Edge!* you will select your favorite character building weapons to help you achieve your personal victories."

Grandmaster Robert E. Beaudoin
World Tang Soo Do Association

"Reflecting on the real experiences of a life journey creates a lot of "learning moments"- Sal shares these in his book. Many will benefit from reading Sal's reflection."

Garry Ridge
President & CEO
WD-40 Company

"Sal has not only mastered the martial arts, but in this book he's mastered the 13 basic principles that have allowed him to find peace and purpose in his life. In today's fast-paced world most people are struggling to find a way to make life's journey more rewarding. Sal provides his recipe for success using his own amazing story as the backdrop. This is a must read!"

L. R. Hering Sr.
Rear Admiral, US Navy (ret)

"As the Coach of the United States Naval Academy Karate-Do Team for the past 22 years, I have trained thousands of students. There are but a handful that have gone beyond the status of student and become family. Sal Convento is one of those unique individuals. He has become an immovable fixture in my family, a role model for my children, and a son to me and my wife. I would wholeheartedly suggest his book to you!"

John Critzos, II, JD
8th Degree Black Belt, Karate Do

"*Black Belt: The Winning Edge!* is an excellent read. Sal Convento's story really captures the essence of how martial arts can transform one's life. I strongly recommend this book to anyone wanting to learn more about the martial way."

Dave Kovar
Kovar's Satori Academy
Founder of ProMAC
2010 recipient of Lifetime Achievement Award, Martial Arts Industry Association

"Sal Convento traces his life's list of accomplishments, and setbacks along the way, with attribution to the martial arts for creating the discipline that kept him on the path towards achieving significant successes in his personal life, martial arts training, and business venture. He explains thirteen "character building life values," intrinsic to martial arts training, that greatly influenced the progress of his journey and asserts that students of any age would receive similar benefits. *Black Belt: The Winning Edge!* is an engaging read for all!"

Bill Strong
8th Degree Black Belt, World Tang Soo Do Association
Assistant Grandmaster

"Sal Convento has Mastered the Art of Tang Soo Do, and is an example of the confidence and self-esteem learned studying the martial arts. He has developed a formula for helping people achieve their dreams and goals. He has used these principles to achieve success on many levels and he shares the steps of this formula in his book *Black Belt: The Winning Edge!* for others to turn dreams into achievements. His book is a great investment in achieving the Winning Edge! in life."

John L. Godwin Sr.
Chief Master Instructor
9th Degree Black Belt, World Sin Moo Hapkido Federation
7th Degree Black Belt, World Tang Soo Do Association

"This exciting book takes you on a path of the American Dream. Even more, it serves as a guide on how to accomplish your dreams. Great lessons lay within!"

Nate Gordon
5th Degree Master Instructor, World Tang Soo Do Association
Author, Nonverbal Behavior in the Martial Arts

"I've known Sal Convento since his days as a midshipman at the United States Naval Academy. He writes with a passion that reveals his soul and he delivers a message about how to achieve greater success that has been tested in the crucible of his life. *Black Belt: The Winning Edge!* is not only about the value of Martial Arts in Sal's successes in life, but also about how it can make you a greater champion in yours."

Captain William T. R. Bogle
USN (Ret), Commandant of Midshipmen, United States Naval Academy 1994-1997

"As a father of two young and very active boys, Sal Convento's United States Karate Academy programs have been tremendous for our children's growth and development. His *Black Belt: The Winning Edge!* philosophy is a very applicable guide for raising kids today. His personal story is compelling, and his 13 principles a great take-away. I've seen our boys thrive under Sal's principles and Karate program, and I recommend every parent read his story and use his philosophy in all they do."

William R. Fenick
CAPTAIN, U.S. Navy

"As a father and an educator, I endorse strongly the valuable advice in *Black Belt: The Winning Edge!* I've witnessed the predictable start, full of enthusiasm, followed by the flagging interest and energy, in my daughters' pursuits of a Black Belt in Tae Kwon Do and my graduate students' personal journeys to a master's degree. This cycle is predictable... and manageable with focus, determination, and courage. This book tells you how to make those qualities a part of your being. It is an easy read, chock full of valuable advice and provides a lifetime of positive impact."

Kurt May
CEO and Co-Founder
Psynomics Incorporated

"Being an Executive Black Belt student myself, and having my three kids enrolled in the program, I am a believer in Sal's philosophies. I wholeheartedly endorse this book for those who want to achieve success in anything in life. Sal Convento embodies 'The American Dream.' "

Allan Camaisa
Ernst and Young Regional Entrepreneur of the Year (Serial Entrepreneur), U.S. Naval Academy Alumni, U.S. Navy Veteran

"Master Sal Convento, and his personal journey into the rich world of Martial Arts, serves as a guiding light for others to find the riches that the Martial Arts have to offer. I believe that this book should be a must read and be a part of every Martial Arts schools library."

Zulfi Ahmed
Founder / Grand Master
Bushi Ban International

"Through this book, I've come to know a martial arts warrior whose beginnings may have been modest, but who, through an incredible display of determination, rose up to demonstrate to his students and to the community he serves, the discipline and sacrifice necessary for great achievement! His actions demonstrate true indomitable spirit. I, for one, am grateful that he serves the martial arts community."

John Cokinos
President Educational Funding Company

"Sal Convento's inspirational story is proof that the American Dream is alive and well! Thanks for the roadmap, and for reminding us that with faith, determination, and a dream; nothing is impossible!"

Mike Schleyhahn
President & CEO
Swagelok San Diego

"I can recommend *Black Belt: The Winning Edge!* for those interested in the martial arts, and for any person who wants to succeed in school, business, and life!"

Christopher Bott
Captain, USN (retired)

Black Belt: The Winning Edge!

Convento

Black Belt: The Winning Edge!
How Martial Arts Can Help You Achieve Greater Success in Life

Sal Convento

ISBN: 1499267460
ISBN-13: 978-1499267464

Convento

DEDICATION

To my wife Kristin

You are the Love of my life. I thank God for bringing us together. I'm forever grateful for your love, support, and making me a better man. I look forward to our bright future and raising our Black Belt children together.

Convento

CONTENTS

Acknowledgements		v
Overview		vii
The Stick		ix
1	My Humble Beginnings and Vision	1
2	The Thirteen Life Values Achieved Through Martial Arts	19
3	Giving Your Child the Gift of Greatness	55
4	No Excuses, Sir!	61
5	The Rewards You Will Find on Your Journey to Black Belt	71
6	Incorporating the Principles of Martial Arts into Your Daily Life	77
7	Becoming a Black Belt in the Business World	83
8	How Martial Arts Can Help You Realize Your Life Purpose	85
	Final Thoughts	89

Convento

ACKNOWLEDGEMENTS

I want to thank Mr. Steve Bouscaren, retired professor of Anthropology, a student at U.S. Karate Academy along with his son Palu, for spending countless hours editing and rewriting this book. The process was long and arduous but worth the time and effort. I want to thank Joseph Guidi, Andrew Baran, Anthony Scoggins, and Adam Brooks for the professional photos in this book. I also want to thank Erik Evans for his editorial and publishing services. Finally, I want to thank my Instructors, Mentors, my staff, students, parents, and my family who unknowingly contributed to my life. You all are my teachers.

Convento

OVERVIEW

My name is Sal Convento. I was born in Manila, Philippines, the youngest of thirteen children. I came to the United States at the age of eight and began my Martial Arts training at age 13. Currently, I am a Fourth Degree Master Instructor in World Tang Soo Do and Fourth Degree Black Belt in Karate Do. I am a two-time World Champion in the art of World Tang Soo Do. I am owner and Chief Instructor of the United States Karate Academy in San Diego, California. I graduated from the United States Naval Academy and served ten and a half years as a Surface Warfare Officer and Naval Aviator. I have a Master's degree in Executive Leadership from the University of San Diego.

This is my personal story of how the Martial Arts became the foundation of my successes. It is based on more than 28 years of Martial Arts experience teaching children and adults. I offer my insights and opinions based on my successes, challenges, and failures of how Martial Arts have greatly impacted my life. My hope is that it will do the same for you.

I want you the reader to know you can achieve a Black Belt! The experience will change your life. I present 13 character-building weapons to help you earn your Black Belt but more importantly, to help you become a champion in life. I share with you the many benefits of a Martial Arts education and training with the hopes that you will one day achieve the rank of Black Belt. I guarantee with 100 percent certainty that with a Black Belt, you will be more disciplined, have greater confidence in yourself, and be better equipped to persevere through life's challenges. Earning a Black Belt helps us as individuals to truly be our best. And, when you are at your best, you become a more productive member of our society. It is my bold vision that all students in America will achieve a Black Belt by the time they graduate high school. I believe this will greatly impact our society.

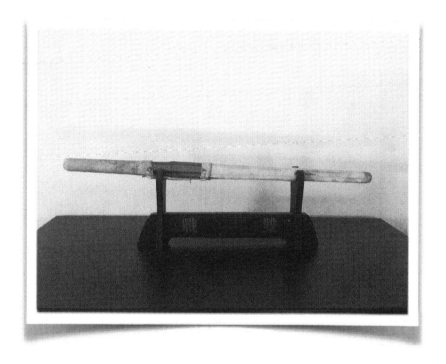

THE STICK

In January 1996, in the freezing temperatures of Annapolis, Maryland, I told my Naval Academy Karate Instructor, Mr. Critzos, I wanted to win Grand Champion in both forms and sparring at the upcoming West Virginia Championship. Rather than telling me "take a hike" or "lower your expectations," he simply stated, "Get ready." The next few months of training would be the most physically, emotionally, mentally, and spiritually demanding of my Martial Arts career.

During a typical sparring session, Mr. Critzos had all the Black Belt students line up according to their skill level with the most experienced, toughest, and well-rested fighter being the last fight of the night. My training session began when Mr. Critzos placed a bamboo stick above my knees. He started swinging the stick back and forth and commanded me to jump higher and higher.

Many times, he would purposely sting me at different parts of my lower body, forcing me to jump higher when my legs grew tired and sore. Then, after a short 30 second rest, he had a well-rested Black Belt spar me for two minutes. After another short rest, came round two, then three, four, five, and sometimes six. They were all the same: the stick followed by a fresh Black Belt.

At one point, I was so physically exhausted I could not bring my arms up to protect myself and one of the Black Belts threw a roundhouse kick to my face. Part of my lower front tooth flew across the floor and I saw it laying on the ground defeated! I was bloodied and exhausted. I couldn't believe what just happened and I was in a state of shock as I picked up my tooth. I walked off the Dojang (Martial Arts training arena), head down. That was the end of our sparring session.

I remember being angry with Mr. Critzos. I asked myself, when is enough enough? I ended up going to the dentist the following day to have my tooth fixed. As I sat in the dentist chair, I wondered how my opponent achieved the upper hand. I knew I had done my best.

I returned the following day, knowing we would start all over again. This time, I was determined to redeem myself. By the fourth or fifth sparring round, when every ounce of my physical being was drained, I had an epiphany. I realized I would need enough mental awareness to keep my hands up! It wasn't so much about my physical state, but my mental state. My training seemed to take over automatically. I entered a state of flow, where my mind naturally defended me from my opponents without consciously thinking about it. I was in the zone.

I realized this was the lesson Mr. Critzos wanted me to learn. When you are physically exhausted, and feel you can't go any further, this is when you must be mentally tougher! You must persevere and allow your mind to take over. This is how you can overcome the challenges you face in the sparring arena of life.

After a few rounds, I was so tired I could barely stand, but I had one last fight to go. I had to spar Lance Burton, the toughest guy in the class. Most of the students feared his speed, strength, and power. He was an experienced and accomplished Tae Kwon Do fighter and wanted to be part of the Olympic fighting team. I knew I had to gain the upper hand by letting my mind take over. When I was physically exhausted, I had to bear down and mentally prepare myself for the toughest fight of the evening. He was well rested.

Lance quickly came out with an aggressive jumping roundhouse kick. At that moment, everything seemed to slow down as if his lightning fast jumping roundhouse kick was instantly played in slow motion. With power and speed, I quickly countered with a spinning hook kick to the face to score a point! Something was triggered within me and I had a natural flow of energy. This was the result of thousands of hours of training sessions. My offensive and defensive movements were an instinctual reaction to his actions. It reminded me of Sir Isaac Newton's third law: for every action there is an equal and opposite reaction. It was an amazing discovery of the power of the mind and its ability to overcome physical weakness.

Through Mr. Critzos' deliberate and intense training regimen, I won many grand champion trophies in forms and sparring during my time at the Naval Academy. I even beat Mark Williams during a sparring competition at the All American Open at Queens College, New York. This was a significant achievement as Mark had been the Sparring Champion at Madison Square Garden numerous times. This was the same tournament where

Mr. Critzos had won the Heavyweight Championship in Sparring five times.

Later, I found out Mr. Critzos only offered "the stick" to individuals who truly wanted to excel in the Martial Arts. You either had to ask for it or he had to see something in you before he would give you the stick treatment. Mr. Critzos had seen how determined I was to win in the Martial Arts arena. The will to win is the same principle I have applied into every facet of my life. This story of the stick perfectly captures the nature of Martial Arts education and training. Once you understand how to apply it, you will have the *Winning Edge!*

Some of the greatest moments of my life were winning in the Martial Arts. The exhilaration of victory and being the best at that moment in time is an indescribable feeling of achievement. Dare to be great! Pursue whatever passion moves you in the arena of life.

CHAPTER 1
MY HUMBLE BEGINNINGS

My beginnings were humble. I was raised in a poor Catholic family in Manila, Philippines, with six brothers and six sisters. I was the youngest of thirteen. We lived in a tiny home where we slept together like sardines in a can. We had only cold water, one no-flushing toilet, no television, a leaking tin roof, and just enough food to live on. I remember when eating rice with salt and water was a meal. My only toy was a stick and my imagination! However, despite all of this, I was constantly aware that my parents' love and support was unconditional. All they wanted was for each of their children to succeed in life. They instilled within us the determination to strive for success. Looking back, I realize how poor we were relative to the

1

American way of living. Despite our lowly beginnings, we were and still are a very close knit and happy family.

My parents were factory workers. Because of World War II, my father never attended school and my mother only had a third grade education. They worked hard throughout their lives and after years of sacrificing and saving, they were able to buy a mango, sugar cane, and coconut plantation. They supported the family from the income they earned on the plantation.

Although we were happy, my oldest brother Bert decided to join the U.S. Navy in search of a better future. After moving to the United States, he began to petition family members one by one. Over a thirty-year period, all my brothers and sisters were finally reunited in the United States.

In March 1981, at eight years of age, it was my turn to come to America. I remember being dressed up in a suit and bow tie when my brother Bernard and I boarded the 747 Northwest Jumbo Jet. I couldn't wait for the plane to take off and land on U.S. soil. I missed my mother Eugenia, and my brothers and sisters who had already taken this life-changing journey to this great land of opportunity called America.

It was during this flight I had my first dream of what I wanted to be! I wondered how such a massive piece of steel could soar through the clouds. As we climbed higher, the buildings and fields below seemed to become nothing more than colorful specks, until they disappeared altogether. The sights of my first flight were awe-inspiring and I remember thinking "I want to be a pilot one day!"

My life and the world around me changed forever when we landed at JFK Airport. We drove to South Philadelphia where my family was living. Our lives were vastly improved. We now owned a car. Our home had hot and cold running water, a flushing toilet, a bed, and a TV. Relative to what we had in the Philippines, I thought now we were "rich!" I was deeply grateful for what America provided us. If I worked hard and stayed focused, I knew there were unlimited opportunities in America.

Despite the improvements, my mom and dad were both on welfare to make ends meet. My mother supported us by working hard at a part-time job that paid $5 an hour at a local sewing factory. But, her pay simply wasn't enough. Yet, she never gave up. She showed us how strength of character and perseverance were valuable traits.

Over the next several years, I learned a new language, made new friends, and adapted to the American way of life. I really felt like I was becoming an American when I joined little league baseball at ten years of age. I had no worries in the world. I went to school, hung out with friends, and had a great time playing the all American pastime. My nephew Gil and I played for the Raiders in South Philadelphia. During my first year, I played many positions but I was best as a pitcher. I wasn't the fastest pitcher but I had great control over my "wicked curve ball" that struck out many batters. At the end of my first season, I was awarded Rookie-of-the Year! This was my first lesson on what confidence can do. I learned the value of teamwork when we won games as a team and not as individuals. I continued to play baseball throughout my high school years learning the value and importance of discipline, hard work, and teamwork. Eventually, my love for baseball would be overshadowed by my passion for Karate.

When I was 13, my brother Bernard and his friend Jay encouraged me to start taking Karate instructions at a local studio in the rough streets of "South Philly." The Karate studio was owned by Grandmaster Jae C. Shin and was called Shin Karate Institute. Grandmaster Shin was the original founder of the World Tang Soo Do Association. Today this Association spans 27 countries with over 160,000 non-Black Belt members, over 15,384 Black Belts, and more than 356 masters. He was mentioned as one of the most influential Martial Artists in the world in the book *20th Century Warriors*. Many years later, Grandmaster Shin would support me in starting my own martial arts studio. He passed away on 9 July 2012.

When I started Karate, I didn't have the same confidence as I did in baseball. Over time, Karate would provide me with the ultimate confidence. My brother Bernard and I trained two hours per day six days a week. Initially, this was for the purpose of having fun, physical fitness, and we thought it was just a cool thing to learn. Then one day, my brother and I were walking in the rough streets of "South Philly" when a group of rowdy teenagers surrounded us at 10th and Oregon on the way to Karate! They started calling us "Chinks" and saying things like "what are you doing walking through my neighborhood." I had hoped they would let us pass but one of the "wise guys" came up to my brother and punched him in the face knocking him down to the ground! They challenged us to fight them but the odds were not in our favor. We left the scene humiliated with bruised egos and heads down. At that moment, we began to look at Karate as a form of self-preservation. We took our Martial Arts training to a higher level by competing at local tournaments. In my first tournament, I cried after losing the sparring competition. Oftentimes, this is when kids will quit. However, this loss fueled my determination to succeed more than a win could ever have done. I vowed to train harder and I set another goal: to win every tournament.

My instructors at Shin Karate were there to support and coach me. They believed I could compete at a higher level and I was determined to prove them right. To prepare for tournaments, Nate Gordon, Louis Castelli, Todd Morrison, and I would get up at 5:00 A.M. to go jogging at the outdoor track at 10th and Bigler in the freezing snow. Two months prior to a tournament, we began to weightlift and spar each other. On top of this, I went to Karate six days a week to work on the basics and the subtle details of each move of the forms, weapons, and sparring techniques. We were committed to being the best. This dedication to excellence resulted in numerous first place wins. Eventually, after earning my Black Belt, I won several Grand Champion trophies in Forms, Sparring, and Weapons at every Tri-State competition. I was fortunate enough to have Karate instructors (Master John Godwin, Louis Marvil, Todd Morrison, and Master Nate Gordon) who taught me to be my best and provided me with the motivation I needed to achieve my goals.

While a freshman in high school, I watched a TV show that would change the direction of my life once again. An episode of Good Morning America with Joan Lunden aired featuring a segment about the U.S. Naval Academy. She discussed the traditions of the Academy, the lineage of families who attended and are currently attending, as well as the superior level of education the institution provided. They described attending the Naval Academy as a privilege and an experience unlike any other. It was known as the most difficult and rewarding college experience in the nation. At that moment, I knew the Naval Academy was the place for me. There were three key reasons for this. First, I would serve my country as a form of gratitude for what America had provided my family. Second, I would be given the chance to become a Navy Pilot to fulfill my childhood dream of flying. And, third, it was free (it was the best education that my parents could afford: FREE!). When I told my Karate instructor, Todd Morrison about my new goal, he helped me prepare for the Academy and supported me every step of the way.

Getting to the Naval Academy was a monumental task in itself. Although, I was an "A" student at Girard Academic Music Program (GAMP) in South Philadelphia, I was not prepared to take the SAT exam during my junior year. I would end up taking the SAT exam SIX times. Did you hear me say SIX times before receiving the minimum score needed to be accepted at the Naval Academy? SIX times!

Prior to taking my first SAT exam, I enrolled in a SAT Prep course. After receiving a combined total of less than 700 (I needed a minimum of 1100 to be accepted), I was completely demoralized! I couldn't even share my test scores with my family, friends, or instructors. I knew I had to take the exam over again. Painfully, I sat through the same SAT Prep Course a second time. This time, I scored just a little better than my first test. For two years as a junior and senior in high school, I attended SAT Prep Courses and repeatedly took the SAT test. But wait, there's more! As a bonus, each test came with a pounding and throbbing headache lasting all day. Even after all this, I believed I was destined to attend the U.S. Naval Academy. It was the only school that fit my personality. I knew it would challenge me to be my best academically, physically, mentally, emotionally, and spiritually. It was the whole person concept. This is why I never gave up. Each time I took the test, I raised my score a tiny bit more. After taking the SAT six times, I finally received a passing score! Now, I thought I would receive my letter of acceptance. Unknown to me, there was another hurdle I had to overcome.

After meeting the minimum SAT requirements, the Admissions Office at the Academy asked me which

Congressman or Senator was nominating me to represent their district at the Academy. Since I was the first to apply to any military Academy in my high school, my counselor had no prior knowledge that I needed a Congressional nomination to the Naval Academy. The Naval Academy recommended I attend college while I pursued a Congressional nomination. I attended the Community College of Philadelphia for one year while I sought a nomination from Pennsylvania Congressman Tom Foglietta. This was a competitive process as each Congressman is given a limited number of nominations to represent their district at the Naval Academy. After three years, beginning with my junior year of high school, taking the SAT six times, attending one year of community college, and receiving a Congressional nomination, I finally received my letter of acceptance to be a Midshipmen to the United States Naval Academy!

This three-year journey was a lesson in perseverance, believing in myself, and not giving up on my dreams. This was the result of complete support from my family and my Karate instructors who were there for me throughout the entire process. When I received the letter of acceptance to the Academy, my family and I felt like we had won the lottery! We were so happy, we cried in joy and gratitude for this great opportunity that would change my life forever. This was a true honor. I believe I would never have been accepted into the Naval Academy without the discipline, confidence, and perseverance from my Martial Arts training. The next four years at the Naval Academy would provide me with more trials, tribulations, and opportunities for success. My Martial Arts training would become more important than ever before.

I began my studies at the Naval Academy in the hot and humid summer month of July 1992. My first year as a Plebe was full of shocking surprises. In high school, I was a big fish in a small pond. I was president of my high school, an honor roll student, and varsity athlete in baseball. So, I arrived at the Academy with big expectations believing I would be an academic stud. In my mind, I saw myself being on the Superintendent's List each semester. This list is more prestigious than the Dean's List in that you needed a 3.4 GPA or higher, an "A" in physical education, and an "A" in Leadership/Military Bearing. This was the whole person concept that measured the entire Midshipmen in academics, physical fitness, and their ability to lead as future officers of the Navy and Marine Corps. At the end of the semester, you were awarded a Gold Star you proudly wore on your uniform. All the other Midshipmen knew you were a "Stud." This award was something every Midshipmen aspired to earn.

During my first semester, I had my basic hard science classes in Chemistry, Math, and Physics. I was used to achieving an "A" in my classes in high school. But, from day one, I realized how unprepared I was academically! Even though I worked diligently as I had in high school, the results of my first semester grades were downright demoralizing! I earned a whopping 1.9 GPA. I was so embarrassed; I couldn't share this news with my family and friends. I asked myself, do I belong here?

On my semester break, I reflected, regrouped, and refocused my efforts on earning "A" or "B" grades for the second semester. I asked my professors for personal extra instruction on various subjects I struggled with during my first semester. After increasing my study time, working smarter "I thought," and having worked with my professors individually, I knew I would raise my grades. Boy was I wrong! My GPA was even lower than the first semester! This time, I was really worried. So, I asked myself another question. Will I ever graduate from here?

On the bright side, upon entering the Naval Academy, every Midshipmen was required to select a sport or extracurricular activity of their choice throughout their four years. Since I had earned my Second Degree Black Belt and was a Regional Champion, I naturally selected Karate. As poorly as I was doing academically during my first year, I was doing the opposite in Karate. I continued to win first place in forms, weapons, and sparring at local area tournaments. But my pride and joy was "Beating Army" in forms and sparring competition in each of the four years I was at the Academy! I taught Karate lessons when needed. Karate was the constant that continued to provide me confidence, a sense of self-worth, belief in myself, a sense of achievement, and room to improve my skills as a leader and Martial Artist. Looking back at this period, Karate was my "fuel for the soul."

My strategy for the second semester was to focus on my academics. At times, I would skip my Karate classes to have more time to dedicate to my "favorite" subjects: Math, Physics, and my all-time favorite "Chemistry!" This is what most people do. We typically give up something that is good for you and spend extra time and effort on what you need to improve. In this case, it was academics. However, it actually hurt me because the benefits of doing the thing I love (Karate) gave me the energy and focus to improve on the subjects that gave me difficulty. Through this experience, I learned spending time in Karate actually helped me to have a clear mind, focus, fortitude, willpower, discipline, and the perseverance to not give up. This was a pivotal lesson in my life.

I realized my strategy for the second semester was not working since my I had a lower GPA than the first semester. From my sophomore to senior year, I changed my strategy to consistently train and compete year after year in Karate. As I devoted more time to Martial Arts training, my skills became more refined, and my grades steadily improved. It culminated in achieving the most coveted Superintendent's List during my senior year! I wore that Gold Star on my uniform with pride and sense of achievement. Karate gave me the foundation to succeed academically and in every aspect of my personal and professional life.

During my first semester at the Naval Academy, I met Mr. John Critzos II. He has become the most influential person in my life. He continues to be the Coach of the Karate Do Team at the U.S. Naval Academy, a program he founded in 1992. He became my instructor, mentor, friend, business coach, and father figure. He had humble beginnings. Growing up he was called "No clothes Critzos" because the other children in his school knew his family didn't have much. Today, he is a successful personal injury lawyer in Washington D.C. He has a beautiful wife and two kids in college. He began training under Ki Wang Kim on 4 September 1973 (see Wikipedia under John Critzos II). Mr. Critzos currently holds an Eighth Degree Black Belt.

We both started Karate at age 13 and are both accomplished Martial Artists. We shared the same beliefs, work ethic, discipline, and passion for the Martial Arts. He made me tougher by instilling the most challenging training regimen I've ever experienced. He consistently emphasized the whole person through the values of Patience, Training, and Character. Not only did he make me a Martial Arts Champion, he showed me how to be a "Champion in Life."

During my senior year at the Naval Academy, I tested for and was awarded my Third Degree Black Belt in Karate Do. While Mr. Critzos was tying on my belt, he told me about passing on the "Baton of Knowledge" to others. He always supported, guided, and mentored me to accomplish my dreams. He supported me in becoming a Navy Pilot and as an entrepreneur. He taught me karate is who you are rather than what you do. It is a way of life that teaches you how to be the person you were meant to be. It will help you to achieve anything you want in life.

During our senior year at the Academy, all Midshipmen select the jobs they want as a career Naval or Marine Corps Officer. I took the ASTB (Aviation Selection Test Battery) as a requirement to selecting Aviation as my career choice. However, I failed to meet the minimum score needed to pass the ASTB. Hmmm... sounds familiar doesn't it? The SAT and the ASTB became the banes of my existence. Since I failed the ASTB, I had to take the long road to Aviation. I had to choose Surface Warfare as a career, get qualified as a Surface Warfare Officer, pass the ASTB, and hopefully be accepted to the Aviation community.

I graduated from the Naval Academy on 24 May 1996. After graduating, my six-month training as a Surface Warfare Officer started at Newport, Rhode Island. Then I moved to sunny San Diego onboard the USS COMSTOCK (LSD-45) as my first duty station. During my two years onboard COMSTOCK, I took the ASTB again and failed it once more. Here we go again.

I had many valuable experiences while onboard the COMSTOCK. The leadership challenges as a Deck Division Officer working with the enlisted personnel made me a better leader. I realized the responsibilities of being a great leader included: leading by example, taking care of the crew, having a personal interest in their personal and professional growth. This practice continues today with my instructors and students. When in port, I trained and taught Martial Arts at a local 24-Hour Fitness gym.

After two years onboard the USS COMSTOCK, I achieved my designation as a Surface Warfare Officer. I was then transferred onboard the USS DENVER (LPD-9) also stationed in San Diego, CA. I was the Main Propulsion Assistant (MPA) in charge of over 100 enlisted personnel and six junior Officers. This provided an opportunity to develop peer-to-peer leadership skills. While stationed on the DENVER, I took the ASTB exam again. This time, on my third attempt, I finally passed the exam qualifying me to attend flight school. The Commanding Officer of the ship (Captain Charles Webber) gave me full support and a letter of recommendation to leave the ship early to fulfill my childhood dream of flying. Throughout this period, I was practicing and teaching Martial Arts onboard the ship while underway and in port.

My journey to flight school was the most difficult path one could take in the Navy. It took me three years longer than someone entering flight school right after graduation. I spent this time on two ships, passed the ASTB, received the full support of my Commanding Officer, and had a lateral transfer board approve my transition to flight school. I was in a rare minority of officers who were accepted to flight school in this manner. The road less traveled gave me more life experiences including enhanced leadership skills, a hard work ethic onboard the ships, traveling to different parts of the world, and all the while never losing sight of my goal to attend flight school.

I was accepted to flight school in 1999 and headed to Pensacola, Florida, the birthplace of Naval Aviation. This is where all student Naval Aviators learn the fundamentals of flying. To me, the rigors of ground school were tougher than the Academy. We had just enough time to absorb the lectures during the day, study in the evenings, and at the end of each week be tested on the material. During this six months of intensive training, I had no time for Martial Arts.

After successfully completing ground school, I was transferred to Corpus Christi, Texas, for training to fly the T-34 Mentor. This is where I learned the basics of aviation, communication, and navigation while learning all the emergencies that can arise in flight. My goal was to fly jets. To do this, I needed a minimum combined NSS score of 50. At the end of my flight training, my combined NSS score was a 49! One point separated me from being eligible to select jets! This is the story of my life. But, I did not give up. I met with the Chief of Naval Air Training (CNATRA) Admiral Boyington, to request permission to fly jets. It was denied. Flying jets for the Navy was one of two goals I did not reach, and could not try again. I was designated a winged Naval Aviator on 25 May 2001 by Admiral Boyington. My family, friends, and mentor John Critzos were present at my winging ceremony in Corpus Christi, Texas. At this momentous occasion, my mother and Mr. Critzos pinned my "Wings of Gold" on my chest. I did well enough to receive my first choice of duty station flying the EP3-Orion out of Rota, Spain. This was a highly sought after duty station. Although I was not flying jets, I had realized my childhood dream of being a pilot!

There were no Tang Soo Do studios in the Corpus Christi area and the bulk of my time was taken by flight training. Before being transferred to Spain, I had training on my new platform in Jacksonville, Florida, where I learned to fly the P-3 Orion. In Jacksonville, I joined a World Tang Soo Do school just outside the Naval Base. I continued to train and teach the students there. It was in Jacksonville, watching the morning news while eating breakfast that the tragedies of September 11 unfolded right before my eyes. Afterwards, I remember President Bush telling all military personnel to "Get Ready!" The events of September 11 changed the way we trained by having a greater sense of purpose. Almost exactly one year later, I was flying missions over Afghanistan in support of Operation Enduring Freedom.

After completing P3-Orion training, I arrived in Rota, Spain with VQ-2 squadron. I was there for approximately two years flying missions from three detachments: Incirlik Air Force Base, the island of Crete, and Bahrain. These missions took eight to thirteen hours with three pilots backing each other. After flying these missions, I began to realize they were not as fulfilling as I thought they would be. I took great honor serving and defending my country. Yet, I felt I was not impacting the lives of the crew in a meaningful way.

Each time we returned to home base (Rota, Spain), I continued to train in the Martial Arts and instruct Karate classes at the MWR (Morale, Welfare, and Recreation) gym to spread my passion of the Martial Arts. It was then I decided to compete at the 2002 World Tang Soo Do Championship in Orlando, Florida. I had the full support of my Commanding Officer, CDR Keith May, to take one week of leave. MWR paid for my airfare and hotel. During this time, I had a detachment in Incirlik Air Force Base. We were restricted to live and train on base due to security concerns. I had to train myself in forms, weapons, and sparring. The biggest challenge was not having a sparring partner. I remember talking to Mr. Critzos about my lack of a training facility and training partners. His remedy was to shadow box with kicking combinations in the corner of the aerobics room at the base gym. I did kicking combinations in the base pool and weight lifted to supplement my training throughout my detachment.

In July 2002, I competed at the World Tang Soo Do Championship with Blacks Belts from all over the world vying for the World Championship Cup in three events. I ended up taking three gold medals: forms, weapons, and sparring as a Second Degree Black Belt! However, another competitor that same year took three gold medals as a Third Degree Black Belt. According to the competition rules and regulations, Rob Masseroni became World Champion in 2002 because he was senior in rank. I came back flying high to VQ-2 a "hero" for representing our Squadron and the U.S. Navy. I was featured in the Rota, Spain, newspaper, All Hands Magazine, and was named European Athlete of the Year for the military!

During my time as a Naval Aviator in Rota, Spain, I faced the difficulties of studying long hours for the next qualification, preparing the next training flight, and studying for the qualification board. I began to realize I was not naturally gifted at learning the various systems of the plane. I was a good pilot but I did not excel at it. This was not due to a lack of effort. I had fulfilled my childhood dream of becoming a pilot. However, it wasn't as much fun and purposeful as I had imagined. In the end, flying did not serve my true talent and calling. All the experiences in the Navy had led me to this point. Each of the values and life lessons I had gathered along the way created this path of defining my true purpose in life. Although, I enjoyed my experiences in the Navy as a Surface Warfare Officer and Naval Aviator, I felt I would best serve my country teaching Martial Arts to children and adults. I excelled in helping others be their best physically, mentally, emotionally, and spiritually through the Martial Arts.

After my tour in Rota, Spain, I came back to my favorite duty station: San Diego, California. I was stationed onboard the USS OGDEN (LPD-5) for two years as Mini-Boss for my disassociated sea tour. During this time, I was actively searching for my first Karate studio location. Simultaneously, I applied to be released from active duty to open my first Martial Arts school. I was denied due to my seven year flying commitment.

I was then sent to my final duty station in Omaha, Nebraska, as Operations Officer at Military Entrance Processing Station (MEPS Omaha). While my first choice was to stay in San Diego, there were no shore duty positions available. At the time, I did not like moving to Omaha but I took advantage of the situation by attending Toastmasters and Martial Arts seminars while going back and forth to San Diego to look for my future studio location. I was also teaching Martial Arts at Offutt Air Force Base MWR gym in Bellevue, Nebraska. With near perfect timing, I received a letter from the Admiral of Navy Personnel offering an early out of my Aviation Commitment and a severance package of a year's pay! Literally, a year before I had written a letter to the same Admiral asking to be relieved from active duty commitment and now they were paying me to get out! This was truly a blessing in disguise. The Navy really took care of me.

In June 2006, while waiting for a suitable location in San Diego, I opened my first U.S. Karate Academy studio in Bellevue, Nebraska. This was the best way to learn the business of the Martial Arts since the rent was inexpensive. In Omaha, I made many mistakes and tried various ideas to see what worked. Throughout this time, I worked my Navy job from six am to three pm. Afterwards, I would teach and manage the Martial Arts studio in the evening. By the end of my tour in Omaha, I felt I had earned my Master's Degree in the business of the Martial Arts. In September 2006, the Navy released me and I began to work full time at the studio.

In March 2007, a space I wanted in the former Naval Training Center (Liberty Station) in San Diego became available. I was in route to Philadelphia for a Martial Arts business seminar, when I received the good news. I immediately canceled my next flight and flew to San Diego instead! What at first seemed like a bad way to end my Naval career, Omaha, had become a great stepping-stone in preparing me for business success. Excitedly, I signed the lease in San Diego. As my Navy life was coming to a close, my purposeful transition to full time Martial Arts instructor and entrepreneur was in full swing.

Looking back I realized I had no control over what cards were dealt to me. Why did I have to take the SAT six times? Why did I have to take the Aviation Selection Test Battery three times? Why did I miss the opportunity to fly jets by one point? Why didn't I get qualified as a 2P pilot? Why was I stationed in Omaha, Nebraska? All of these challenges could be seen as negative circumstances in my life. However, I made conscious decisions to not be a victim of circumstances. In each of these situations, I had the freedom to choose to make the most of what I had been dealt, not give up on my dreams, and come out a better person. These choices led me to my career in the Martial Arts.

My Vision

I want my students to be more successful than I have been. I attribute my accomplishments to the application of my Martial Arts education and training. Knowing this, I have a bold dream and vision that one day every student will graduate high school having earned a Black Belt! There are four parts to this vision. First, all parents with children in a professional Martial Arts studio will take their children's training as seriously as their formal education. This would mean every child will graduate with a Black Belt. Second, Martial Arts are recognized as an optional sport from elementary grades through high school as it is at the U.S. Naval Academy. This would be an after school program for students to choose among the variety of sports the school offers. Third, Martial Arts would be part of physical education from elementary grades through high school like other sports such as swimming, boxing, gymnastics, wrestling, and judo. These are all required graded classes at the U.S. Naval Academy. Fourth, Martial Arts classes will be a required part of the curriculum from elementary grades through high school. Students will start in kindergarten and continue until they achieve Black Belt. In this four-part vision, we would see children as young as 10 years of age up to high school ages earning the rank of Black Belt.

If you are a parent who isn't quite sure if enrolling your child in Karate to earn a Black Belt is a worthwhile endeavor; I can tell you, it is. If you are a professional such as a lawyer, doctor, or CEO of a company, or the average person who doesn't know how Martial Arts can positively impact your life; I can tell you, it will. This book is meant to show you how the Martial Arts can help you attain true success, and more importantly, significance in your life. By having a Black Belt mentality, you can achieve your life's goals and dreams.

The character values discussed below are the foundation of my success. My hope is for the readers of this book to implement these values into their own lives. By using these values, you will "Be Your Best!" By being your best, significance will come to you as it has for me. Practitioners of the Martial Arts are armed with 13 character-building weapons. By being a modern Martial Arts Warrior, you will defeat the enemies from within, conquer the highest mountains, and feel the exhilaration of victory!

CHAPTER 2
THE THIRTEEN LIFE VALUES ACHIEVED
THROUGH MARTIAL ARTS

"Victory is reserved for those who are willing to pay its price."
Sun Tzu

In ancient times, practitioners of Martial Arts trained their bodies to be weapons against enemies. The enemies we normally think of are like those the Navy Seals face in combat. Today, Martial Artists practice self-defense but also emphasize a true warrior has conquered the enemies from within. In life, we normally don't encounter our traditional enemies. But, we all have enemies from within. Today, the enemies include but are not limited to obesity, lack of exercise, lacking a sense of purpose, alcoholism, drugs, smoking, and financial challenges.

I believe any form of Martial Arts is the most effective way to fight these enemies from within. Martial Artists are armed with 13 character-building weapons. These are: Discipline, Confidence, Perseverance, Integrity and Strength of Character, Commitment to Excellence, Dedication, Leadership, Teamwork, Passion, Goal Setting and Achievement, Flexibility and Adaptability, Vulnerability and Reflection, and Mentorship and Passing on the Baton of Knowledge. Martial Arts training arm us with these weapons to defeat our enemies.

Martial Arts have the power to instill several life values. Regardless of your age, financial standing, or gender, you have the opportunity to learn a variety of teachings through Martial Arts. Many people believe Karate is merely designed for self-defense. It can do much more! It is an education of the self in every way. It offers you the chance to become your best. It provides you with all the tools needed to create success and fulfill your life's purpose. For that reason alone, Martial Arts must be a required part of life's curriculum just as Mathematics and English are in our schools.

Character Building Weapon Number One: Discipline

"Discipline is the bridge between goals and accomplishment."
Jim Rohn

Discipline is doing the things you have to do, whether you feel like it or not. All the goals I have accomplished in my life resulted from taking action towards achieving them on a daily basis. Discipline is the beginning of success. Of the thirteen weapons, Discipline is first and foremost. With Discipline, you will positively influence the people around you.

I start each morning with a rigorous physical workout. I make my bed, followed by a good breakfast, and on my travel to work I listen to educational or inspirational audiobooks. This disciplined approach to simple tasks centers me for the rest of the day. It prepares me to do the most difficult tasks first thing in the morning when I'm most mentally alert and physically strong. This is respecting myself.

Not being Disciplined is easy. Look at the world around you and see the increasing number of obese kids and adults. This is the result of choosing the path of least resistance. Many people lack the Discipline to eat less and exercise more. I say choose the path of most resistance. At first, everything is difficult. However, the more Disciplined you get, the easier it becomes. Discipline becomes part of you. It becomes habitual and automatic. Jim Rohn said, "We must all suffer one of two things, the pain of Discipline or the pain of regret or disappointment." I have chosen the pain of Discipline and it has brought me joy and happiness in the accomplishment of my dreams.

When I was a full time graduate student at the University of San Diego, I was running a full time Martial Arts business. I had to take a disciplined approach to complete my Master of Science in Executive Leadership. In addition to my normal routine, each morning I spent a minimum of two hours studying. With this routine, I was able to earn A's in most of my classes. The discipline required to get A's in graduate school is the same discipline needed to achieve excellence in Martial Arts. This is why I believe the study of Martial Arts is education. It requires the same Discipline to achieve higher levels of success.

Character Building Weapon Number Two: Confidence

"Go confidently in the direction of your dreams!
Live the life you've imagined."
Henry David Thoreau

Our ability to take on life's challenges depends greatly upon our level of Confidence. The more Confidence we have, the more successful we can become. If we allow circumstances to diminish our Confidence or the actions of others to chip away at our self-esteem, then we cannot become the successful individuals we were meant to be.

Ever since I was a child, I've worked towards the accomplishment of my goals and dreams. I wanted to be a pilot, attend the Naval Academy, be a teacher of the Martial Arts, and I'm in the process of becoming a more successful Martial Arts business owner. I have accomplished these things with Confidence. What gave me the power to achieve these goals is the Confidence from within. This is primarily from my Martial

Arts training. Confidence is gained when you have competence in what you are doing. Competence is gained when you possess the required skills and knowledge with a dedicated time and effort. Confidence is what made me take my savings and risk it all in opening a studio. I did this because I was Confident in pursuing the life I imagined.

The three biggest risks in my life, going to the Naval Academy, becoming a Naval Aviator, and going into business for myself, made me who I am today. Starting my own business allowed me to share with others the talents and skills I believe are essential in life. The Confidence you get from Martial Arts training, winning in competition, being physically fit, and knowing you can defend yourself, is the foundation for Confidence building. When you have Confidence, you can do anything, have anything, and be anything you want to be.

In the Martial Arts, we are always testing ourselves. Through training, we learn how to overcome life's challenges. Each of us was born with our own potential set of skills and talents. Training the mind and body allows us to sharpen those skills and build upon them. This leads to higher levels of Confidence and self-esteem. With renewed Confidence, we become individuals with greater potential. You will have the ability to go after your goals and dreams without hesitation. With Confidence in yourself, your dreams will one day become a reality!

Character Building Weapon Number Three:
Perseverance

"Champions are not made in gyms. Champions are made from something they have deep inside them: a desire, a dream, and a vision. They have to have last-minute stamina, they have to be a little faster, and they have to have the skill and the will. But the will must be stronger than the skill."
Muhammad Ali

Martial Arts teach the importance of never giving up, regardless of the situation you face. There is always a solution to a problem. If you dedicate the time needed to learn the skills required, you can overcome any obstacle. Martial Arts provide the practitioner the confidence you need to Persevere through difficult times, even when the challenges seem overwhelming. The teachings give you the power to triumph where others have failed and better yourself as a result.

Throughout my 28 years of Martial Arts training, there have been goals and achievements I wanted so much I would have done anything to accomplish them. If I had simply waited for these things to happen, or let obstacles stand in my way, I wouldn't be where I am today. I wouldn't be writing this book to stress the importance of Martial Arts as an education. Simply put, without Perseverance, I would never have achieved my goals. Perseverance has given me the opportunity to make something of my life and become a better person. For this, I am grateful to Martial Arts.

A story of Perseverance comes to mind. When I was in flight school, there came a time when I was given the opportunity to select flying Navy Jets (F/A 18 Hornets or F-14 Tomcats), propellers, or helicopters. After watching the movie Top Gun, I'd always wanted to be part of this prestigious and elite group. At the time, I thought these fighter pilots were cool, confident, and were the best of the best. I gave 100 percent effort on every test and flight with the goal of eventually becoming a fighter pilot.

During each flight, our flight instructors would grade us on specific skills such as emergency procedures, knowledge of plane mechanics, and situational awareness in the air. The grades were above average, average, and below average. At the end of flight training, all students were given a comprehensive score (NSS). Based on the NSS score, I could choose to fly jets, propellers, or helicopters. This score was comprised of ground school and flight school. At the end of this training period, I received a score of 49. The minimum score needed to select jets was 50! Oh, so close. Unlike all the previous tests I had taken such as the SAT and ASTB, this test CAN NOT be taken again and again because student aviators cannot repeat ground school and flight school just to improve their score. Although I had fulfilled my childhood dream of flying, I always wanted to be the best in whatever field of endeavor I chose. Naturally, I wanted to fly jets. Even after missing the required score by one point, I did not give up.

I am not one who backs down easily. I went around and asked all of my fellow naval aviators, my instructor pilots, and anyone else who I thought might be willing, to write a letter of recommendation. I was determined to get into the fighter pilot program, and thought maybe, just maybe, enough letters would convince the higher-ups I was good enough. After gathering all of the recommendations, I finally received notice to see Admiral Boyington, Chief of Naval Air Training in Corpus Christi, Texas. He had the final authority to change my fate. At the time, Admiral Boyington was the "GOD of Naval Aviation." He was the highest-ranking Admiral I had the pleasure to interact with during my entire naval career. I was so nervous to meet him. Armed with my letters, I prepared my speech well in advance and went into his office with confidence. He listened to me while I pleaded my case, and then the Admiral spoke.

The first part of his response got my hopes up. He acknowledged my Perseverance, confidence, belief in myself, and my dream of flying jets! However, his last sentence made my heart sink. From his years of experience in Naval Aviation, he spoke with authority and wisdom. He denied my request based on his experience that the lower the NSS score the lower the chance of graduating from the Jet program. I left his office completely devastated. I couldn't believe all my hard work had not led to a positive outcome. I cried that day. It took me quite a while to overcome this humbling defeat. And, that was that. "The God of Naval Aviation had spoken." Maverick was shot down and killed that day! R.I.P. Maverick. Flying jets for the

Navy was one of two goals I did not reach and could not try again. I had reached the limits of Perseverance.

Though this story might not seem like it has a happy ending, I earned my first choice of duty station, Rota, Spain. This was the most sought after duty station for propeller pilots because I did well in ground and flight school. I enjoyed my life in Spain and have had a life filled with opportunities ever since. If I had become a fighter pilot, who knows where my path in life may have taken me. Even when I suffered a major defeat, I had the Perseverance to keep going. I chose to keep my dreams intact, even though they had been altered. I didn't let this failure get in my way.

People do not begin a Martial Arts education because it is easy. They start because they know it will challenge them. Those who have earned the Black Belt have learned the long-term benefits of Perseverance. While those who have not, may have squandered opportunities for greater success. When you dedicate your time and effort to Martial Arts, you will learn that obstacles are merely ways to improve yourself and become a complete warrior.

Character Building Weapon Number Four: Integrity and Strength of Character

"This above all: to thine own self be true,
And it must follow, as the night the day,
Thou canst not then be false to any man."
Shakespeare

Integrity is defined as adhering to moral and ethical principles. It is the state of being whole and can be used to describe a ship's hull. At the Naval Academy, starting at the beginning of Plebe summer, it was instilled in us that "Midshipmen do not lie, cheat, or steal." This is what most people think of when you mention the word Integrity. You must be true to yourself, your team, and your organization.

In Martial Arts, we learn about Integrity through the physical aspect of the form. For example, when a ship has a small hole, it starts to leak water into the ship. Over time, the hole gets bigger and eventually the ship sinks to the bottom of the ocean. In doing forms, your foundation is in the perfecting of your stances, blocks, kicks, and strikes over time. The more precise and detailed the technique, the better the structure of the form. This translates into a stronger foundation with even greater Integrity. When the physical Integrity of the form is excellent, this transfers to your daily dealings with life. When practicing your form at your best, you are working towards becoming a complete person. Giving your best effort makes it difficult to lie, cheat, or steal from yourself and others. When you are a person of Integrity, others will see you as trustworthy and honorable. The Integrity you gain from your Martial Arts training allows you to Be Your Best.

At the United States Karate Academy in San Diego, our instructors regularly hold "mat chat" sessions, where we stress the importance of the whole person concept through Integrity. We teach it in the physical sense, by focusing on how one can build an excellent form. The Integrity of your form depends upon whether your form has holes in it, or is whole. We ask students to determine where they see weakness in their form and we encourage them to strive for excellence within that form.

The subject of Integrity reminds me of something that frequently occurs in reference to practicing forms. I stood in front of one of my youth classes, and decided it would be a perfect opportunity to make a point about taking pride in your form. I showed the students an example of a sloppy form, wherein I didn't concentrate on my movements or my stances. I, basically, showed them forms lacking Integrity. I then asked them to tell me what was wrong with my form. Right away, the students picked up on the fact I was not paying attention to the details of my form. I wasn't giving it my best and it wasn't a good example of what I could really do. I told them they were right and replied: if I was not watching you, would you give it your best? Each of them shook their head and told me they could give it their all without me observing them. They knew they were responsible for their own actions and a sloppy form was not going to reflect well on their Integrity.

Choosing the path of least resistance is easy but does not allow you to nurture your Integrity. In essence, Martial Arts teach you everything you do should be done with conviction and the utmost Integrity. Only actions and words carried out with great thought and dedication are going to reflect your true honor. It teaches you no matter what life holds for you, you should be true to your principles and morals. This way, you can always be an example for others to follow. With Integrity comes Strength of Character.

Strength of Character

"The ultimate aim of Karate lies not in victory nor defeat, but in the perfection of the Character of its participants."
Gichin Funakoshi

Strength of Character is not something that happens overnight, nor is it a trait we are born with. If you come into contact with someone who exhibits a strong sense of Character, you can rest assured they have invested a great deal of effort into improving themselves. They have used each of the values mentioned in this book to rise above obstacles and used the lessons to carry out continual self-improvement.

Throughout the course of our lives, we are building Strength of Character. Each of the actions we take or decisions we make add to our Character. Martial Arts allow us to build our Strength of Character by instilling confidence and a sense of purpose in each of us. It stresses the importance of learning discipline in order to become the individual you truly want to be regardless of your past or current situation.

Martial Arts empower you with the tools to take on the challenges of life. Having a true sense of Character enables you to soar above the negativities of life and challenges you will encounter. Even those who were dealt a rough hand have the chance to become their best so long as they continue to develop their Strength of Character. It is overcoming the struggles and failures we experience that build our Character. It is these struggles and failures that make you appreciate who you are, what you have, and what you are doing. When others fail or give up early, the individuals who stay the course continue to build their Character like eagles soaring above the mountaintops.

The stick story illustrates an important aspect of Character building. It was the most physically challenging Martial Arts training I had ever experienced. You become so physically exhausted you cannot keep your hands up to defend yourself from your opponent. It is at this point when Character building occurs in that you have to increasingly rely on your mental faculties to "stay in the fight." Mr. Critzos would say, "as your physical strength rapidly declines you must increasingly rely on your mental fortitude to keep fighting." This is the beginning of Character building. The stick, that simple bamboo stick, served to be a significant building block of my Character. It is a symbol of the struggles each of us must go through in life. While some of these struggles might seem insurmountable at the time, we must fight on, not quit, and allow for the tests to give us Strength of Character.

Character Building Weapon Number Five: Commitment to Excellence

"We are what we repeatedly do.
Excellence, then, is not an act but a habit."
Aristotle

Martial Arts teach its students that we are all a work-in-progress. I've lived my life based upon the "CANI" principle. CANI stands for Constant And Never-ending Improvement. The Japanese know this philosophy as Kaizen for continuous improvement. We are all creatures of habit, and everyday each of us has the opportunity to get rid of bad habits and replace them with habits of Excellence. Every day we must strive to become better than the day before, and do more to reach our personal and professional goals. Martial Arts help us to understand we can always reach higher levels of Excellence in and out of the Dojang.

The discipline of the Martial Arts has ingrained in me that Excellence is practicing every technique over and over and over again with exacting detail. Excellence is not a one time or sometime thing, it is an all-time thing. It does not magically happen overnight, and it cannot happen at all if we are not actively pursuing Excellence in everything we do. When I train for competition, I practice the most difficult part of the form over and over. I would do this until it became second nature. I won the World Championship two times because of this attention to the most insignificant of details. Implementing small changes and little improvements on a daily basis gradually builds to an insurmountable difference over time. This is the difference between winning gold or silver.

In my Martial Arts classes, I stress the importance of proper form and making movements instinctive like breathing. When my students are practicing their techniques, they are accustomed to hearing me say, "do it again." You have to do something over and over and over again if you want to achieve Excellence. It's not the most exciting thing, but the rewards you receive will come later on when you compete and win medals. This is true in life. The rewards may not be immediate, but your investment of quality time and effort will eventually yield the success you desire with a life of Excellence.

A Commitment to Excellence requires a change of perspective. Martial Arts have taught me to strive for the best to provide others an example of Excellence at every level. It is my responsibility to ask my students to have the same level of Commitment to Excellence. This is a radical shift in perspective, especially when you compare it to the mindset many of us have today. Most people go through life simply getting by instead of thriving. They settle for less from themselves and from others. Rather than trying to achieve more and do better, they have grown used to mediocrity. I've met many people who want the Black Belt now, but do not want to put in the time and effort it takes. This is the mindset of many Americans today. Rather, choose a life of Excellence.

Martial Arts will teach you how to have a Commitment to Excellence. Once you have learned the importance of being your best all the time, there is no limit to what you can achieve. Dedicating yourself to Martial Arts allow you to witness how a Commitment to Excellence can improve your Martial Arts training and be a driving force behind your journey to Black Belt.

Character Building Weapon Number Six: Dedication

"Practice isn't the thing you do once you're good. It's the thing
you do that makes you good."
Malcolm Gladwell

Dedication is investing a great amount of time to some
purpose. Without Dedication, all the values I mention in this
book would mean nothing. It takes a great deal of Dedication to
follow through with our passion, to achieve our goals, and to
pursue a Black Belt in life. Without an unwavering Dedication to
achieving our goals, we would give up and never reach our true
potential. Those who are willing to Dedicate themselves fully to
Martial Arts will have the *Winning Edge!* inside and outside of the
Dojang.

I'm reminded of the Dedication necessary in accomplishing
my goals such as graduating from Annapolis, flying for the Navy,
and having a successful business. Each required a great deal of
Dedication. Winning the World Championship is an excellent

example of Dedication. Fellow Martial Artists would come up to me assuming I was a natural athlete and Martial Artist. They were envious because they thought I possessed natural skills in Martial Arts. Even though I have some natural physical abilities, I am not a natural born Martial Artist. The talent and skills are a result of countless hours of Dedication to being the best I can be.

In his book, *Outliers: The Story of Success,* Malcolm Gladwell repeatedly mentions the "10,000 hour rule" claiming the key to success in any field is, to a large extent, a matter of practicing a specific task for a total of around 10,000 hours (Wikipedia: *Outliers: The Story of Success,* 2008). After consistently training for more than 28 years to be the best in Karate Do and Tang Soo Do, I have crossed the 10,000 hours threshold. Are you willing to Dedicate countless hours needed to achieve greatness? This is Dedication!

Students of the Martial Arts must dedicate their mind, body, and spirit to training. Then, and only then, will they be able to be their best at whatever they choose to do. They have made the conscious decision to give it their all, rather than settle for mediocrity. These individuals have come to the realization that only through Dedication can one hope to achieve greatness.

Character Building Weapon Number Seven: Leadership

"A Leader is best when people barely know he exists, when his work is done, his aim fulfilled, they will say: we did it ourselves."
Lao Tzu

To be a great Leader, you must first be a great follower. I began my followership as a lowly white belt. I followed my instructors and those senior to me in rank. As a follower, you learn the basic skills and teachings of the Martial Arts. You do not question the authority, direction, and experience of your instructors. The foundations of my Leadership skills were heavily influenced by my instructors and mentors who taught me to Lead by example. While you can learn from both a bad Leader and a great Leader, having a great Leader will propel you to achieve more in life.

After one year of studying Tang Soo Do, I earned my Brown Belt and began assisting in classes by Leading the warm up. This was my first Leadership experience where I was accountable to others. All eyes were on me to guide and direct the entire class. When I became a Black Belt, I earned the privilege to teach all students from white belt to Black Belt. As a Leader, you exude authority and influence over those you teach. In the Dojang, I never ask anyone to do anything I'm not willing to do. I realized being a strong Leader required me to both act and look the part by having excellent techniques, being physically fit, and more importantly, being a person of good moral character.

Before you can Lead others, you need to learn how to Lead yourself. You are in control of your form. You are in control of how well you do in your sparring match. You are in control of whether you win or lose. Ultimately, you must first Lead yourself to success. While you must be willing and able to take direction from your teachers, you are the only one who can take action to make your dreams come to reality. Only you can take responsibility for your actions and decisions, which makes Leading oneself an essential value in every aspect of life. Once you have mastered the art of Leading yourself, then you are in a position to Lead others.

When reflecting upon your life, you will undoubtedly find you have been impacted by those who have Led you in some way. Leadership is a core value in life. It gives each of us the ability to learn from someone with more experience to Lead others so we may pass on that which we have received. Therefore, becoming a Leader in some aspect of life is crucial to our personal and professional growth.

Character Building Weapon Number Eight: Teamwork

"On the strength of one link in the cable,
Dependeth the might of the chain.
Who knows when thou may'st be tested?
So live that thou bearest the strain!"
Captain Hopwood, R.N. (Laws of the Navy)

Martial Arts are quite often viewed as an individual "sport." When people think of Teamwork, their thoughts turn to team sports like football, soccer, and baseball, but not Karate. Martial Arts have the power to teach every student the value of working together as a Team better than most "activities" synonymous with team building.

Martial Arts emphasize the importance of collaboration. You must work with others on your Demonstration Team to have the same rhythm, movements, and stances as those of your Teammates. You learn more can be accomplished as a Team than as an individual.

An excellent example of how Martial Arts have instilled this value within me was when I was part of a Demonstration Team that won gold in the creativity competition at the World Championship. Ten of us worked together diligently. We practiced tirelessly on weekends to perfect the creative part of our routine timed to music. Our hard work paid off and we proved to ourselves what we could accomplish. First, we worked on our individual parts. Then those individual parts came together to form the bigger group routine. What began as an individual effort became a strong and united Team. Only when you have done your best as an individual, can you be an effective and contributing member of the Team. The Team is only as strong as the weakest link.

I would not have attained the goals I've set throughout my life without a group of dedicated individuals who believed in my dreams and what I wanted to achieve. Whether it was to get into the Naval Academy, flight school, or starting my own business, I relied heavily on a Team of people to help me make the wisest decisions. Martial Arts taught me the value of Teamwork in life, not just in the Dojang. The person I look at in the mirror is a compilation of my family, friends, supporters, and mentors who have helped me along the way. I stand upon the shoulders of giants who have gone before me, who have helped me reach my goals sooner by avoiding the "minefields" of life.

If one is dedicated, their Martial Arts training will help them identify their strengths and weaknesses. This will help them create a Team that uses those strengths and minimizes the weaknesses to achieve any goal. Through the Martial Arts, I have learned we need to work together as a Team to make our individual and collective goals become a reality.

Character Building Weapon Number Nine: Passion

"To achieve all that is possible, attempt the impossible, to be as
much as you can, dream of being more."
Martin Luther King, Jr.

Passion is the thread that binds us together. Every great
endeavor can only be attained when we have a burning desire to
do whatever it takes! Passion is the fuel that gets you up before
the rising sun, and the driving force that enables you to have the
energy required to achieve a purpose greater than yourself.
Passion is what drives the soul. Without it, we would not have
the capacity to become our very best, and would not be able to
achieve the goals that are possible.

Passion is a powerful tool that gives you the ability to turn
each of your dreams into tangible realities. Through my Passion
of the Martial Arts, I have come to realize my life purpose. My
life purpose is to use my leadership skills and expertise in the
Martial Arts to inspire and teach children and adults to be their

best by being physically fit, mentally sharp, emotionally stable, and spiritually sound in order to have productive citizens of our great society. This is the Mission of the United States Karate Academy. And, this is how I want to be remembered. When I am gone, my dream will live on, thanks to my Passion. It is my ambition to have the headstone upon my final resting place read: "Sal Convento...August 26, 1972...2072...Here lies a man who was a great husband, father, and Master Martial Artist who spread the Passion of the Martial Arts for the greater good of mankind."

What are your dreams? What are you Passionate about? Are you willing to do whatever it takes to see your true Passion become a reality? Martial Arts will give its dedicated practitioners a very unique gift: a Passion for achieving your full potential. The Martial Arts can show you how to use Passion to "Be Your Best." This in turn helps others to find the Passion in their lives. Passion sustains and enables you to be truly happy and fulfilled in your life.

Without Passion for life, learning, and for achieving excellence, even the most determined among us cannot hope to achieve our wildest dreams. While Passion may not be taught in our society on a regular basis, it is a value that is essential to our success, and is continuously spread through the Martial Arts.

Character Building Weapon Number 10: Goal Setting and Achievement

"No one can predict to what heights you can soar.
Even you will not know, until you spread your wings."
Unknown

Goals are targets to achieve with a certain deadline. The idea of Setting Goals has become something of a cliché featured in every business, motivational, or self-help book you see today. There are very few disciplines in life that can give an individual the ability to Set and Achieve Goals like the Martial Arts.

Students of the Martial Arts set small Goals on a daily basis. Each training session is an opportunity to Set and Achieve a Goal. Whether it is to learn a new movement, or to improve our form, a big part of Karate is Goal Setting and Achieving on a continual basis. Martial Arts teach that the cycle of Goal Setting is never ending. Once you have Achieved a Goal, you Set a new one to improve yourself.

Each of us is a work-in-progress. Goal Setting gives us the opportunity to progress on a daily basis in pursuit of the perfection of our character. With each Goal we Achieve, we are made better for it. It's not the Goals you accomplish that empower you to become a more complete person, but the lessons you learn along the way in Achieving the Goal.

There are many ways to reach our Goals. The reward you receive from Achieving your Goal is not the Goal itself but what you become in the process of Achieving the Goal. I won the World Championship twice in two different age categories. I wanted to prove it could be done and I wanted to be the first to accomplish this feat. I told myself I would do whatever it took each day to ensure I had done everything possible to reach my Goal. I dedicated countless hours to training in and out of the Dojang. I followed a strict diet, weightlifted, ran, sparred, and practiced my forms over and over again to exacting detail. Although I am proud of my accomplishments, the real prize was what I gained in the process. In the end, I became more disciplined, gained greater confidence, had a higher level of self-esteem, stronger willpower, earned more respect, increased belief in myself, had excellent health, and led my students by example. This is what you become when you Set and Achieve your Goals in life by doing something every day towards the attainment of your dreams. Are you willing to pay the price to Achieve your Goals?

Character Building Weapon Number Eleven: Flexibility and Adaptability

"It is not the strongest or the most intelligent who will survive but those who can best manage change."
Charles Darwin

Being Flexible and having the ability to Adapt is just as important as having conviction and dedication. While you may have a plan of what you want out of life, who you want to be, and a time frame within which you want to accomplish your dreams, you must have the Flexibility to roll with the punches life will throw at you. Without this Flexibility, you will not make the most of the obstacles you will face nor the lessons they will offer in an ever-changing world.

While I was in the Navy, I quickly learned I would have to master the art of Flexibility and Adaptability. For example, every one and a half to two years I had to move to a different location. This involved moving everything I owned, looking for a new home, and Adapting to a new environment. Regardless of the location, I discovered how to make the best of it.

I was fortunate to have lived in Rota, Spain, and Omaha, Nebraska. These are two completely different worlds. I loved Spain, the year round warm weather, the breathtaking beaches, quaint small towns, and the friendly people. However, being in the Navy meant I would have to move sooner or later. I was relocated to Omaha as my last shore duty assignment. Omaha, Nebraska, was very different from Rota, Spain. It had difficult winters and no beaches. Rather than sulking about my new duty station, I chose to make the best of the situation. I attended seminars on the business of Martial Arts and participated in Toastmasters. Instead of having a negative view, I took the time to build my business skills in Omaha and opened my first studio there. The rent was cheap, and it was in Omaha where I implemented the ideas I learned in seminars.

In Martial Arts, being Flexible and Adaptable to different situations is emphasized again and again. Being physically Flexible allows the practitioner to have fewer injuries, have an arsenal of techniques, and therefore Adapt to an opponent more readily. Every opponent you face has different strengths and weaknesses. You must be able to adjust your form, your movements, and your stance to overcome your opponent. If you are facing a new opponent in the sparring arena, you must change the strategy to defeat the opponent. If you simply carry out the same strategy with different opponents, you are going to be defeated. You must be Flexible and Adapt in order to flourish in an ever-changing environment.

Character Building Weapon Number Twelve: Vulnerability and Reflection

"To share your weakness is to make yourself Vulnerable; to make yourself Vulnerable is to show your strength."
Chris Jami

Perhaps the most surprising weapon used to defeat the enemy from within is Vulnerability and Reflection. I had always thought of Vulnerability as weakness. Now, I see it as strength.

During flight school, I thought my biggest failure was not being selected to fly jets for the U.S. Navy because I failed to qualify by a single point. Nonetheless, I became a Naval Aviator and flew the EP3 Orion out of Rota, Spain. My real failure, however, was not getting qualified as a Second Pilot (2P) at my Squadron.

Let me explain. When I was stationed in Rota, Spain, my main job was to get qualified as a Pilot In Command. Once you achieve this qualification, you have the complete trust of your Commanding Officer to fly missions anywhere in the world with a crew of 23 military personnel. The order of qualification is Third Pilot (3P), then Second Pilot (2P), and eventually the Pilot In Command. On a typical military mission flight, three pilots were required to fly missions that normally took 8 to 13 hours. I easily passed the 3P qualification since it was the basics of flying, landing, and emergency procedures without getting into the technical part of the systems. To pass 2P qualification, I needed to know the systems such as the inner workings of the propellers, electrical systems, radars, emergency procedures, and how everything was interrelated. To test for 2P, we had an oral board with three senior Pilots In Command who knew the systems inside and out. I studied long and hard for this test since I knew this was my weakness.

I failed the first test and the board recommended I retake the qualification at a future designated time. I studied by myself and with other pilots seven days a week knowing my fate as a Naval Aviator rested on this board. When I had the oral board for the second time, the senior pilots asked me the same questions as before. I had memorized the answers but did not understand how everything truly worked. I failed the oral board for the second time. Don't misunderstand me; it was not for lack of trying. My Commanding Officer and Executive Officer knew I had spent countless hours preparing for the oral board. I gave it my best effort but I had reached my mental limit.

I realized the significance of this failure meant I would never fly the EP-3 Orion again. I felt inadequate, stupid, and not good enough. Even though I had a great support group of junior aviators, I felt like I did not belong. This was the lowest point of my entire naval career. For the first time ever in my life, I was beyond Vulnerable. I was so embarrassed and felt so small that prior to this writing, I had only told two people about this low point in my life.

Reflecting back to my time in Spain, it was then I asked myself, "what am I doing?" Yes, it was my childhood dream to fly but the reality is that it was not my calling. At the same time, I realized I have always been an excellent Martial Artist. I realized teaching Karate is my true calling and that teaching others what I know best serves a higher purpose.

After being sent back to San Diego early because I did not get qualified, I continued to serve my country with my remaining time commitment. I knew not qualifying for 2P was a career-ending situation for me. Staying in the Navy for the remaining 10 years to get retirement pay was not desirable knowing I would not fly again nor move up through the ranks. In my free time, I began to transition into the Martial Arts in search of opening my own Martial Arts Studio. Karate has always been my strength and now I wanted to make it my profession.

Sometimes it takes failure to teach you the lessons in life. Out of failure comes Vulnerability and out of Vulnerability comes Reflection. Out of Reflection comes inner strength and out of inner strength comes the power to start life anew.

Character Building Weapon Number Thirteen: Mentorship and Passing On the Baton of Knowedge

"If I have seen further it is by standing on the shoulders of
giants."
Isaac Newton

I am a product of the many instructors who have helped me get to where I am today. My achievements thus far would not be possible without the support, guidance, and coaching of the Mentors who believed in the power of my dreams. I continue to rely upon them to show me the way, and encourage me to be my best. I now have the opportunity to do the same for others. Karate shows you how to become a student first and teacher second. Just as my instructors helped me to be my best, you will become a Mentor to others and help them be their best.

I currently have two mentors in my life. One is my Martial Arts business Mentor, John Godwin, who was my first instructor in South Philadelphia. He has the distinction of being the most successful business owner in the World Tang Soo Do Association to date. He has over 1000 students and six Martial Arts studios. My second Mentor is John Critzos II, who has been a second father figure, instructor, mentor, and friend. Both men have been there during the special events in my life. They helped me see further in life by providing me priceless advice. They guided me through the challenges of life without any major setbacks. Thanks to their constant support and motivation, my personal life and business have benefited greatly.

I have relied upon the support of my peers as well. You need to have peers in your life, as they will hold you accountable for your actions, maintain healthy competition, and sharpen your skills. In addition to being Mentored, you should always Mentor someone who is less experienced than you to help them succeed. This reminds you of your earlier ambitions, goals, and reignites your inner passion. Teaching the knowledge you have learned reinforces that knowledge and is the best form of learning. And now, you have come full circle. When you have been Mentored by someone who has enhanced your life, it is your responsibility to pass this Baton of Knowledge on to others.

Passing On the Baton of Knowledge

During my senior year at the Naval Academy, I earned my Third Degree Black Belt in Karate Do. At the ceremony, while receiving my belt, Mr. Critzos handed me the stick he had used during my entire time at the Naval Academy. This was the "Baton of Knowledge" his instructor, Ki Whang Kim, had passed on to him, and Mr. Critzos was passing it on to me. Mr. Critzos said to me: "I've given you just about everything I could give you, it is now time to pass it on to others." I understood to honor Mr. Critzos and my other instructors, I had a responsibility to take the Baton of Knowledge and pass it on to others.

I continue to pass on the knowledge I've learned from Martial Arts since I was a Brown Belt. I believe we should learn as much as possible, but more importantly implement that knowledge for positive gain. Sharing our experiences, advice, and life lessons with others will give us personal satisfaction and benefit others by helping them be their best.

We will all be teachers at some point in our lives. Parents are teachers to their children and children are teachers to their friends. As teachers, we influence the people around us in both positive and negative ways. This is why we need to be a positive role model. What a wonderful opportunity to share the knowledge others have shared with us. My instructors' advice and knowledge, when applied, helped me become who I am today. You have the power to transform someone's life during your own lifetime, and you should consider it to be a privilege and an honor to do so. Take an interest in someone and pass the Baton of Knowledge on to that person. You will change their world!

CHAPTER 3
GIVING YOUR CHILD THE GIFT OF GREATNESS

"By constant self-discipline and self-control you can develop greatness of character."
Grenville Kleiser

Although I am not a parent, I have spent thousands of hours teaching kids as early as 18 months to teenagers on becoming a Black Belt. What I found is that those children that are successful in formal education and achieved the rank of Black Belt have one thing in common: engaged and supportive parents.

As a parent, you want to give your children the best life possible and provide them with opportunities for a better future. You want your children to have more, do more, and be more than you could ever have dreamed for yourself. You encourage them to do their best in school, be healthy, and instill in them the values you believe are important in order to become productive members of society. While parents are brainstorming the various ways they can give their children the best chance of succeeding in life, achieving a Black Belt in the Martial Arts may not be at the forefront of their minds. What enters the minds of most parents is "why don't we have our child try Karate and see if he/she likes it?" What enters my mind when I hear this, as I relate this thought to formal education is, "let's have our child try second grade and see if he/she likes it?"

Very few parents realize Martial Arts can offer their children a competitive edge in their formal classroom education and, more importantly, in life. It helps them develop skills that reinforce the curriculum of traditional schools such as discipline, confidence, perseverance, dedication, focus, and integrity. In Martial Arts, our unique approach is teaching these character traits from a physical level initially, and then to mental, emotional, and spiritual levels. On their journey to Black Belt, children will be given the opportunity to learn core values they can use to achieve their true potential. Each Karate class is designed to teach respect, honor, integrity, and the other character values mentioned in this book. It goes beyond what other sports provide and enables them to be physically, mentally, emotionally, and spiritually sound individuals.

Their ability to focus is improved and they become more determined to do their best in school. This allows them to excel in school so they can go on to follow whatever career path they choose. Children who learn Martial Arts don't settle for less than excellence in school. There is a strong correlation between having achieved the rank of Black Belt and being a straight "A" student. Children with Black Belts have well-developed social skills, a heightened sense of awareness, and are street smart, as well as book smart.

As an instructor, I consider it an honor and privilege to play a key role in influencing the lives of the children who walk through the doors of my Dojang. I have been there to see them achieve victories inside and outside the sparring arena, and to encourage them when they face defeat. I have always stressed how Martial Arts provide the opportunity to test one's mettle, regardless of age, in an environment that is supportive, safe, controlled, and educational. I have been fortunate to have several of my students, both children and adults, earn their Black Belts and two of my students go on to become World Champions.

I have also spoken with parents who are not willing to make their children go to Karate class when they don't feel like it. "My son/daughter doesn't feel like coming to class today" is something I hear frequently. I often reply to these parents by asking if they would make their children go to school if they "didn't feel like it." The parents always answer with a resounding "yes, of course," to which I say, "Well, Martial Arts is a form of education, so why wouldn't you make them come to class, even if they are not necessarily in the mood for it today?"

I wonder where I would be today if I decided to stop going to Martial Arts classes when I was younger. What if I had "not felt like going today?" This is how I felt at times during my training.

I went to class anyway. This built my discipline and willpower. As a parent, it can be difficult and challenging initially. Over time with support and encouragement, your children will overcome their initial resistance, build their discipline, and eventually enjoy the classes as they become more comfortable with the environment. I can say, without a doubt, my life would not have been filled with the blessings and opportunities I enjoy today if I had been allowed to quit. Taking this path has allowed me to be my very best. I have to give thanks to my mentors and parents as they instilled in me that giving up wasn't an option. I knew I had to persevere and stay focused, so I could succeed.

Parents tell me the main reason they bring their children to class is to learn discipline. While every child has free will, children rarely understand what is best for them, especially in terms of learning discipline. Kids just want to have fun. They don't want to learn discipline. Therein lies the challenge we face on a daily basis as Martial Arts instructors, to teach discipline in a fun way. Many parents understand that teaching discipline to their children today will be an important tool to help them in the future. So, the parents have their kids "try" Martial Arts for a short time and then allow their kids to quit when they are bored and move on to another activity. When the child begins to struggle, most parents do not stay the course. By following this course of action, the parents allow their children to make the decision about what is best for them because many parents do not want to fight this battle. By letting their children win, it begs the question, who is in charge? The parents are teaching their kids it is okay to quit when things get tough. We have become a society accustomed to instant gratification and mediocrity. Most parents don't understand that earning the rank of Black Belt is like graduating from high school. By graduating as a Black Belt, the student has learned the fundamentals to succeed in life just like in high school. Children must be offered guidance and support from the very beginning and be encouraged to continue to the rank of Black Belt. This will ensure children a brighter future and give them the *Winning Edge* in life.

It's also important to mention how Martial Arts can benefit children who suffer from behavioral problems such as ADD (attention deficit disorder), ADHD (attention deficit hyper disorder), and even Autism. Karate encourages a calm focus and enables children to get a better sense of self in a setting that offers stability and respect. They must concentrate on their form and their movements, paying careful attention to detail in a structured environment. These children are better equipped to overcome challenges and gain an enhanced sense of self-control.

The privilege to teach Martial Arts has been a double-edged sword. I have seen countless children miss out on the opportunities Karate can provide. Their parents may have let them quit early because they were unaware of the benefits their children would gain by achieving the rank of Black Belt. This is the main reason I chose to write this book. Many parents view Martial Arts as an activity or a sport rather than an education for their child. I disagree. Likewise, I cannot tell you how many times I have heard a parent say they "just don't have time for Martial Arts" or "their child is in too many activities already." Parents provide their children the gift of greatness by encouraging, supporting, and engaging their children to continue their Martial Arts training to achieve the rank of Black Belt. However, many parents think of Martial Arts training as a part time activity and when it becomes difficult, it's time to quit. When we do this, we are teaching our kids that it's okay to quit when things become difficult. I am making a bold statement when I say parents must not give their children the option to quit Martial Arts just like they do not have the option to quit the second grade! Most parents not only want their child to graduate from high school but better yet, college. They realize how important higher education is by providing their children with the tools to succeed in life. You are teaching them that the battle to "Be Your Best" isn't easily won, but is worth every ounce of effort you put into it. By encouraging your children to continue their Martial Arts training and education through the rank of Black Belt, you are giving them the gift of greatness for the rest of their lives!

CHAPTER 4
NO EXCUSES, SIR!

"It is wise to direct your anger towards problems - not people;
to focus your energies on answers - not excuses."
William Arthur Ward

As owner of the United States Karate Academy, I've been privileged to teach countless students how Martial Arts can help them to achieve success in their lives. I have met with many "success hurdles" along the way. These hurdles are a nice way of saying "excuses." I want to dispel them once and for all.

1. "My child is bored and fights me when it's time to go to class. We want to quit."

This is the excuse I hear most often from parents and puzzles me the most. If your child was "bored" with school, would you allow them to stay home? Most likely, your answer to this would be "absolutely not!" It is not a choice. Since any form of Martial Arts is education, why wouldn't you make your child go to Karate class? They have no choice. It is not an option. While it is required by law to send your kids to school, you don't need a law requiring you to send your child to a Martial Arts studio to achieve the rank of Black Belt. Having the education that comes with earning a Black Belt will always give your child a competitive edge in life. So, why wouldn't you want to provide this lifelong advantage to your child?

I know the easy way out is to have your child get their way, which instantly gratifies the child and yourself. Kids will always choose fun over discipline. To some kids, physical activity is hard work. Children do not know what is best for them and are shortsighted. But a parent who gives in now, will have to deal with more difficult challenges later. If you allow them to quit, you are teaching them that if they do not like something, just cry and complain to get what they want. So the parent is easily swayed to give in for the short-term instant gratification rather than the long-term benefit of delayed gratification.

If you want them to receive the benefits Martial Arts offer, encourage them to stick with it to Black Belt. Earning the Black Belt will help them to advance in life and achieve greater success in the process.

2. "I'm too out of shape for Martial Arts. I probably wouldn't be able to keep up with the rest of the students."

Initially, yes, it's going to be a little tough. It is difficult to learn new skills. It will be a little challenging at first until you become more physically fit and build up your stamina. The more you attend classes the more physically fit you become. The Dojang is a supportive environment. No one is going to criticize you for being out of shape, or judge you for being overweight. All I ever ask of my students is they do their best and train at their own pace. You don't need to lose weight before you start Karate. Karate helps you lose weight. There always has to be a first step if you want to improve your life. If you want to "Be Your Best," starting Martial Arts training can be your first step on your path to getting in shape.

3. "I can't afford Karate lessons. I'm on a budget, and I just don't have the money set aside for Martial Arts."

Many people believe Martial Arts training is primarily physical exercise and compare this to exercise gyms such as 24 hour fitness for $20 per month. Practicing the Martial Arts does include physical training but it is so much more. It is personal development in the highest sense.

Karate is an investment in training and education. My total investment in the Martial Arts from the ages of 13-18 including tuition, testing fees, uniforms, gear, and tournament costs was approximately $10,000. As a result, I learned the values of Discipline, Confidence, and Perseverance. While these values are not easily measured in dollars and cents, they provided me the foundation to attend and graduate from the U.S. Naval Academy with a four-year education worth more than $180,000. This was a direct benefit from my Martial Arts training.

To this day, Martial Arts continue to save and make me money in ways that cannot be easily quantified such as having excellent health and no vices such as smoking, drinking, gambling, and drugs. All of these have saved me thousands of dollars. Throughout my training, I was surrounded by mentors who helped me make the right decisions in life. These are the main benefits of my Martial Arts training. Is this worth it? Without hesitation, I would reply with a resounding Yes!

Martial Arts teach you the "yes you can" attitude. If there's a will, there's a way. At the U.S. Karate Academy, if you want to earn the rank of Black Belt bad enough, money aside, we will do everything in our power to help you afford the tuition.

Recently, we started a non-profit organization called Kicks For Kids to provide scholarships to help defray the cost of tuition, tournaments, and associated activities for students who are financially challenged. We are actively looking for donors who believe Martial Arts training and education are keys to success and want to help others reach their full potential.

4. "We are so busy...I don't think I have time for Martial Arts" or "Both my partner and I are working, and neither of us have the time to bring our child in for classes."

Everyone is busy. But are you busy investing time, money, and effort into the things that will improve your life? The activities kids are busy doing include: soccer, baseball, football, gymnastics, dance, piano lessons, and swimming to name a few. These activities teach motor skills, social skills, individual, and team effort. Parents often want their children to quit Karate to pursue other endeavors. When you quit Karate, you lose what you have learned. Prior to quitting, parents should consider how much Martial Arts will complement these other activities. While we do not discourage students from participating in other activities, we recommend Karate as the foundation of them all. Karate teaches focus, physical stamina, perseverance, confidence, and the discipline to do whatever it takes to succeed in any arena. Unlike the other activities, which are seasonal, Karate is year round.

A major difference in Karate is the end goal of Black Belt. Very few children will become professional in other activities but all children can achieve Black Belt. The problem many parents face when it comes to Martial Arts is dealing with delayed gratification. The rewards are not immediate. With each rank attained on their way to Black Belt, you will see increased confidence, discipline, and improved physical fitness in your child. Black Belt is something that keeps on giving while other activities stop.

5. "My child is too young for Martial Arts and I'm too old."

At the U.S. Karate Academy, we instruct children as young as a year and half. We call them Diaper Dragons since some start while they are still in Diapers. They learn to listen, pay attention, and follow directions. The mom, dad, or nanny is with the child the entire class to help corral the wild Diaper Dragons. The Diaper Dragons start learning social skills and show respect to others by bowing. Their parents model good behavior by teaching their children the importance of fitness. Keep in mind swimming classes usually start as early as six months, so why not Karate? If they can run or swim, they are old enough for Karate.

For the mature crowd, they typically do not participate in Karate for the following reasons: lack of stamina, age related injuries, and some believe karate is for the younger population. The point of Martial Arts is anyone, in any age group, can participate in Karate at their own pace. It's about healthy living and improving one's quality of life. Karate is geared toward constant and never-ending improvement.

Recently, we had an 84-year-old man with multiple injuries successfully test for First Degree Black Belt. I have a 66-year-old female student with osteoporosis successfully test for First Degree Black Belt. She competes and wins at the Regional and World Championship levels. She now has osteopenia, which shows improvement in her medical condition primarily due to her prescribed medication combined with her Martial Arts training. Lastly, I have a 52 year-old female student with arthritis on her knee win the Female Senior Gup Champion at the 2012 World Championship and successfully test for First Degree Black Belt. The limits you face are those you place upon yourself.

6. "I don't want my child learning how to fight. Besides, doesn't Martial Arts promote violence?"

I hear this excuse every now and then, and it is one of the biggest misconceptions about Karate. No, Karate does not promote violence. To the contrary, kids have used the confidence gained from Martial Arts training to avert physical altercations. Kids do get excited when they learn to kick and punch for the first time. Some may get overly excited about it and want to show off their moves on the playground or when they are with their friends. They won't do it in a violent manner, but are merely excited they have learned something new and want to share it.

On the few occasions this has happened, I've always arranged a meeting with the parent, child, and myself to talk about it. I stress it is disrespectful, and the movements they learn in the Dojang should be used only for self-defense. I've never had a child continue to "show-off" once we have the talk.

7. "I've never done any type of sport before, and I don't think I'm coordinated enough for Karate. Karate is too difficult and I'm not very athletic."

We all start out uncoordinated in any physical activity. It takes time, effort, and dedication to become coordinated. With repetition and consistent training, Karate makes you physically coordinated because it makes use of your entire body.

If you are determined to become a Black Belt, you will succeed. It's not about how athletic you are, but your determination to achieve your goal. Muhammad Ali said it best, "it's not the skill, but the will" that truly leads to success. I've met many students who start as White Belts with no coordination and skill become Champions because they dedicated lots of time and effort to be their best. As with all worthwhile endeavors, achieving a Black Belt in Karate is worth the investment in time, money, and effort.

8. "I have an old injury. I don't think Martial Arts training is such a good idea because I might aggravate it."

Studying the Martial Arts like any physical activity can result in injuries. Martial Arts are not supposed to give you injuries. In fact, they can help you avoid future injuries by making you more physically fit, aware of your body, and flexible. Martial Arts teach you how to perfect your form and pay attention to each of your movements thereby reducing the chances of injury.

In Martial Arts classes, you don't have to go full on if you have an injury. You can work on other things, like your forms, techniques, and break down every move to its finer detail. You can do things in slow motion until you recover, and even improve upon your Martial Arts skills while healing in the process.

9. "I probably won't ever have to use Karate in real life. I don't see the point in learning Martial Arts."

Whenever I hear this excuse, a quote from Master Gichin Funakoshi comes to mind: "The ultimate aim of Karate lies not in victory or defeat, but in the perfection of the character of its participants." In short, the ultimate warrior will not have to use their weapons, but will have the restraint and discipline to draw upon the teachings learned during his or her Martial Arts training and education. Since I began training in the Martial Arts at age 13, I've never used physical Martial Arts to defend myself. In my early twenties, I did use my confidence to diffuse a situation that could have escalated to an actual bar brawl.

10. "I don't want to fight Black Belts in my class. One of the main reasons why I've been avoiding Martial Arts classes is because I'm afraid I'll get hurt."

Among all the practitioners of the Martial Arts, Black Belts are the most skilled and have the most control. They can be intimidating knowing they can hurt you with the skills they possess. However, it is the beginners with little skill and control who are more likely to hurt other students during practice. In our Dojang, we stress safety as a priority especially during sparring and self-defense sessions. If you have a profession that uses your hands such as Dentistry, we give the student the option to not spar. However, part of Martial Arts is facing your fears.

You have to be able to face whatever is holding you back and overcome it.

11. "I'm not really comfortable in group settings, and I know Martial Arts classes usually involve training with other people."

Most Dojangs offer private lessons. You will benefit greatly from one on one feedback from your instructors. However, what's great about group classes is the socialization, mentoring, motivation, and encouragement a group setting can offer. Like most physical activities, it's always more fun to do it with a group of dedicated practitioners. In group training, you gain the ability to spar with different people and learn from their experiences.

Also, a necessary part of life is being comfortable doing what's uncomfortable. Being uncomfortable shows you are growing and learning. If being in a group setting makes you a bit uneasy, think of it as an opportunity to face your fears.

CHAPTER 5
THE REWARDS YOU WILL FIND ON YOUR JOURNEY TO BLACK BELT

"A Black Belt is nothing more than a belt that goes around your waist. Being a Black Belt is a state of mind and attitude. "
Rick English

Accomplishing the goal you are trying to achieve is not really the reward. Instead, the journey in achieving the goal is what truly provides you the benefits. The same is true for your journey to Black Belt. After passing the series of tests to earn the honor of wearing the Black Belt, it is the gifts you receive in pursuit of the Black Belt that have the power to change your life in ways you may not have imagined.

Those who have achieved their Black Belt have become warriors with discipline, confidence, and perseverance required to earn this distinction. These character traits are developed and honed throughout the journey. Wearing a Black Belt enables you to show you have sparred to the best of your ability, trained tirelessly, and are continually willing to perfect your form. A Black Belt is a symbol of what you have achieved in the process.

I believe the Martial Arts give you the power to be as good as you want to be as long as you are willing to devote the time and effort necessary. Earning the Black Belt and being able to wear it proudly represents your hard work and dedication. The Black Belt is a sign you have excelled where others have failed.

The same can be said for those who have truly succeeded in life. Only people who have taken the time to learn about themselves will have the opportunity to be their best. Physical and mental hurdles must be overcome, and challenges must be faced with the greatest humility and resourcefulness.

Earning a Black Belt in the Martial Arts will mean something different for everyone who embarks upon the journey. Some may acquire the strength to face their fears and overcome them. Others will discover they can push their physical boundaries further than ever before. One thing is true for everyone striving for Black Belt: it will enhance every aspect of your life.

This is true for those who are already physically fit, the young and the old, and even those who don't really believe Martial Arts have the power to make a significant difference in their lives.

Martial Arts transcend boundaries and transform your outlook on life as you journey to the rank of Black Belt.

Many of us go through life without ever being physically, mentally, emotionally, or spiritually tested. Few disciplines possess the power to do this. When we protect our children and ourselves from failure, we lose the opportunity to learn the lessons Martial Arts provide. Through failure we learn how to improve ourselves and become winners. Through this process, the goals we thought were unreachable are now possible. Martial Arts provide this learning opportunity to push your limits in a safe and controlled environment where you discover your true potential. Practitioners of the Martial Arts are better prepared for real life challenges with a shield of confidence.

Martial Arts allow you to take the road less traveled by testing your mettle on your journey to Black Belt. There are many other advantages gathered along the way. Here are a few of those benefits:

Stress Relief. It's no secret stress runs rampant today. More of us suffer stress related illnesses than ever before from stress at home and work. The number one way to fight negative stress is a physically demanding work out. Martial Arts give you the power to reduce your levels of stress by learning how to better face challenges that come your way. Karate provides you with the physical outlet you need to "let off some steam" improving your overall well-being.

Improved Confidence. The best way to improve your confidence is to be physically fit. Secondly, competence builds your confidence. The competence you gain from being a Martial Arts practitioner gives you confidence in your daily life. Martial Arts provide you the opportunity to prove you have what it takes to "Be Your Best." Once you surpass your mental limits, you can take on anything.

Enhanced Physical Ability. Regardless of your current physical fitness, Martial Arts will improve both your physical abilities and mental acuity. In order to advance on the road to Black Belt, you will be required to test yourself and your skills on a daily basis. Becoming a Martial Artist is a lifestyle conducive to physical well-being that complements other physical activities you enjoy. It will bring your game up to a higher level. Your Martial Arts training will give you a sense of youthfulness and vitality as you mature.

Achieve your Goals. Achieving Black Belt is one of the most physically demanding endeavors you can attempt, as well as one of the most rewarding. If you can do this, you will be a member of a small group of special people who earned the Black Belt. On your journey to Black Belt, you will take yourself out of your comfort zone. This can lead to endless possibilities. When you earn a Black Belt so much is demanded of you physically, mentally, emotionally, and spiritually. With a Black Belt, you can be sure you have the tools to accomplish anything you want to be, do, and have in life.

My entire Martial Arts career is comprised of experiences that turned out to be once in a lifetime opportunities. My journey to Black Belt has had many highs and some lows which have made me who I am today. Being accepted to the U.S. Naval Academy, becoming a Naval Aviator, being a two-time World Champion, having a successful Martial Arts studio, and earning a Master's Degree in Executive Leadership are the results of my Martial Arts training.

Earning my First Degree Black Belt was essentially the master key to achieving the successes in my life. Earning the Black Belt gave me the road map on how to succeed in any endeavor. It has opened many doors for me because I am disciplined, confident, and persistent. I have been taught what it takes to be a true warrior. Once you know how to become a true warrior, no one can take it away from you. It will forever keep giving back since you know what it takes to succeed. This is why I believe every student needs to graduate from high school with a Black Belt in Martial Arts. It will give them the *Winning Edge* in life.

CHAPTER 6
INCORPORATING THE PRINCIPLES OF MARTIAL ARTS INTO YOUR DAILY LIFE

"If you always put limit on everything you do, physical or anything else. It will spread into your work and into your life. There are no limits. There are only plateaus, and you must not stay there, you must go beyond them."
Bruce Lee

The teachings Martial Arts offer extend far beyond the Dojang. Everything you learn from your Instructor will serve you in your daily life. Even teachings that may seem insignificant, such as perfecting your form, instill within you values like patience, focus, and attention to details useful in everyday life. As a result, when you are dedicated to your Martial Arts education and training, you will realize the power to improve your quality of life and make you a more complete individual.

There's a story that comes to mind whenever I think about Martial Arts in relation to our everyday life. A few years ago, someone walked into the Dojang and wanted to know what I could teach them. Besides self-defense, what other benefits can be gained from Martial Arts education and training?

This concern is one I have to address every now and then, but this person stands out in my mind. She seemed determined to dispute each of the key benefits of Karate. When I tried to explain how Martial Arts could help her be more successful in her personal and professional life, she made up an excuse about Karate "taking time away from her pursuit of success, rather than helping it along." When I told her about the core values Martial Arts provided, she responded by saying she could learn those values elsewhere in a way that was much easier and not as physically demanding. Every reason I gave her for enrolling in Martial Arts was met with negativity and a well thought out excuse of why it would not work for her.

Finally, when I was almost sure nothing was going to influence this woman's perception of Martial Arts, I told her:

"Training in Karate isn't easy, you're right. It challenges you mentally, physically, emotionally, and spiritually. But nothing worth achieving in life is easy, is it? You have to work hard to make a living, to excel in your career, and to balance your personal and professional life. All of these things are worthwhile endeavors. Karate is the same. The benefits you will receive on your way to Black Belt will help you in every aspect of your life. If you can overcome obstacles in the Dojang, you have the power to overcome any challenges that come your way outside of the Dojang. You test yourself and push your limits while striving for Black Belt in ways you haven't done before. The education and physical training you receive will be demanding and challenging, but so is life."

The woman looked at me for a minute, not saying a word. I don't think she was expecting me to take the time to address her reasons for not beginning Karate classes. Then, after all of those doubts had been addressed, she signed up for Martial Arts classes on the spot. Later, after she started experiencing the "real world" benefits Karate offered, she told me she had not been aware how Martial Arts training would apply beyond the Dojang. Like many people, she thought Martial Arts are only for self-defense. Now, she uses Martial Arts in everyday life.

Here are just a few ways that you can begin to incorporate Martial Arts into your daily life:

- Overcome Challenges with a Martial Arts Mindset.
The mindset of the disciplined warrior will overcome all challenges. Your "enemy" will be defeated. I will overcome. Karate equips you with the skills you need to look at a problem from every possible angle. Martial Arts teach you to look at adversity by breaking it down into small and manageable pieces. All of us encounter problems every day, having a warrior's mindset enables you to put your problems into perspective and have the best outcome possible.

- Emotional Stability.
The Martial Arts teach every practitioner how to be cool, calm, and collected during stressful situations, instead of being

"emotionally hijacked." Remaining emotionally stable allows you to face your problems with clarity. During your Martial Arts training, you are placed in physically demanding workouts. This positive stress placed on your body will allow you to fend off negative stress in a manageable fashion. In sparring, we are taught to see our opponent's strengths and weaknesses and compare them to our own. We then devise a plan of attack that will ensure victory. Mentally seeing the advantages and disadvantages of my opponent and myself, allows me to see how best to defeat my enemy. This is the same for defeating any challenges you may encounter.

- Get Rid Of The "Monkey's Back."

There are medical reports which state obesity has reached epidemic highs among children and adults in the United States. Millions of people are suffering from being overweight. I call this the "Monkey's Back." The result of this is low confidence, low self-esteem, lack of energy, mental fatigue, emotional challenges, and spiritual lows that will take you to the hospital with diabetes! The opposite is true when you get rid of the "Monkey's Back" by shedding unwanted pounds. You will have greater energy, confidence, self-esteem, and a healthier lifestyle that lands you a trip to Bora Bora with the beautiful body you deserve. Martial Arts help you become physically fit and active on a daily basis. This, in turn, allows you to enjoy life to the fullest without being held back by physical limitations and constant fatigue.

- Be an Effective Leader and a Cooperative Team Member.

Undoubtedly, each of us will find ourselves in situations throughout the day requiring us to either lead or follow. Martial Arts instill within you the power to be an effective leader, one who can guide their team through any project or situation, as well as being a cooperative team player. Both of these attributes are often required in and out of the workplace.

I have been training in Martial Arts for the majority of my life. While I have seen thousands of practitioners benefit from studying the Martial Arts, I've also seen thousands of people whose lives would be better if they were training in the Martial Arts. I sometimes find it challenging to see how others are not realizing the true benefits of Karate. It's often difficult to understand the other end of the spectrum. Many people fail to grasp the idea that the study of Martial Arts is one of the best forms of personal development. Martial Arts give you the tools to help you succeed in your daily life.

CHAPTER 7
BECOMING A BLACK BELT IN THE
BUSINESS WORLD

"If you'll not settle for anything less than your best, you'll be
amazed at what you can accomplish in your lives."
Vince Lombardi

Martial Arts and the business world go hand-in-hand. All of
the values Karate teaches can help you to excel in your
professional life. I offer an exclusive program called "Executive
Black Belt" designed to help working professionals and

83

executives achieve the rank of Black Belt in the comfort of their home or business in the shortest time possible. I've designed it for those executives with busy schedules who want to pursue the Martial Arts training and education. I offer one-on-one personal instruction tailored to their wants and needs. I provide this unique program because I understand Karate can be of immense benefit to those who lead an executive lifestyle.

Of all the weapons Martial Arts arm us with, there are three I use every day: the Discipline to do the things you have to do whether you feel like it or not, the Confidence that comes with competence to believe in the realization of your dreams, and the Perseverance to try again and again when you fail. Martial Arts stress the importance of teamwork and developing oneself as a leader. All of these qualities are essential given that those who are self-assured are more prone to business success.

As any business owner or entrepreneur will openly admit, you will only achieve your true potential through hard work and sacrifice. You must persevere and remain steadfast on your path to success when others have failed and given up. While countless individuals have chosen to take shortcuts in achieving their goals, you have chosen the path that is less traveled and more rewarding. This is the essence of Martial Arts. There may be easier ways to get physical activity, but these ways do not offer you the discipline to excel in life. Only with Discipline, Confidence, and Perseverance will you overcome obstacles that stand between you and Black Belt. The same is true in the business world.

CHAPTER 8
HOW MARTIAL ARTS CAN HELP YOU TO
REALIZE YOUR LIFE PURPOSE

"Let others lead small lives, but not you.
Let others argue over small things, but not you.
Let others cry over small hurts, but not you.
Let others leave their future in someone else's hands,
but not you."
Jim Rohn

On the surface, Martial Arts may appear to be nothing more than a means of self-defense. After all, much of its instruction is

85

centered on mastering kicks, punches, forms, achieving excellence in the sparring arena, and studying combative techniques. This is one of the biggest misconceptions about Martial Arts. Martial Arts are not merely a resource you can draw upon to protect yourself, but a way to discover your true purpose in life.

I feel fortunate I was able to begin Karate at the age of 13. I was taught I could achieve anything as long as I believed in myself. My instructors taught me that with discipline, perseverance, and the drive to achieve, nothing was out of reach. This allowed me to strive for excellence in every aspect of my life. It also gave me the opportunity to realize my true potential and a sense of purpose greater than myself.

At its core, Martial Arts enable us to connect with ourselves. Karate provides us the opportunity to gauge our strengths and weaknesses. Each time I entered the sparring arena, I was asked to test my abilities and to push myself further than I had before. With every new opponent, I proved to myself I could do better than before and raised the bar to a higher level. While receiving my education in Karate, I learned to be master of myself. This led me to choose Martial Arts as a profession.

It's important to understand many of us go through life without realizing we are just getting by, rather than thriving. We place ourselves in boxes from which we never quite escape. The fear, hesitation, resistance, and lack of drive we develop over the course of our lives prevent us from becoming the person we want to be. Think about how many people haven't realized their true potential in life by not living to the fullest. How many of us are not using the gifts and talents we are given because we are afraid to fail?

Karate enables you to break through the barriers holding you back. It teaches you that your mind and body can become one by centering yourself. This allows you to do things you thought were impossible. In today's busy, technology centered world, it can be difficult to take the time to search within yourself. Many people fail to "dig deep" and ask themselves what they should be doing to give their lives a greater sense of purpose. We all have to-do lists that are not necessarily headed in the direction of our purpose. We go through the motions, plugged in to our mobile devices and computers unable to see the higher purpose. In the hustle and bustle of every day life, we lose ourselves. We lose sight of our goals. As a result, we are unable to realize our true calling.

People frequently tell me they don't have time for Martial Arts. I know Karate can help them be more productive by having a sense of clarity, focus, and energy to use their time more efficiently to serve their purpose. It is not something that hinders you on the road to success, but a way of thinking and being that helps you overcome any challenges standing between you and your life purpose.

FINAL THOUGHTS

I began training in the Martial Arts at the age of 13. Now, more than 28 years later, I can honestly say Martial Arts have "Changed My World!" The journey to achieving my Black Belt was the catalyst that ingrained in me the Discipline, Confidence, and Perseverance to "Dare Greatly." Who would have imagined that a poor Filipino kid playing the stick game on the streets of Manila, the youngest of thirteen children, would graduate from the United States Naval Academy, fulfill his childhood dream of becoming a Naval Aviator, become a two-time World Champion, earn a Master's Degree in Executive Leadership, and own a successful state of the art Martial Arts studio in San Diego. And, the journey continues "to achieve all that is possible..." All of my achievements can be attributed to earning my Black Belt as a result of my Martial Arts training and education.

But I'm not unique. You can accomplish your goals. Martial Arts have given me the great opportunities to be my best and to never settle for anything less than excellence. There is not a day that goes by I don't use the teachings Martial Arts have provided me. These teachings are the weapons I use to conquer the enemies from within to change myself, my family, and our community and as a result, the world we live in.

These weapons are: Discipline, Confidence, Perseverance, Integrity and Strength of Character, Commitment to Excellence, Dedication, Leadership, Teamwork, Passion, Goal Setting and Achievement, Flexibility and Adaptability, Vulnerability and Reflection, and Mentorship and Passing on the Baton of Knowledge.

I am forever grateful for the education and training I have received from every one of my Instructors and Mentors over the years. Earning the Black Belt gives you all the tools you need to accomplish great things in your life thus giving you the Winning Edge!

This is why I firmly believe every child needs to graduate high school with a Black Belt so they can be their best. I am, after all, passing on the baton of knowledge as my mentors did for me. If this book helps one person earn their Black Belt then I have indeed helped to change the world. I leave you with this last quote.

"I Wanted To Change The World"

When I was a young man, I wanted to change the world. I found it was difficult to change the world, so I tried to change my nation. When I found I couldn't change the nation, I began to focus on my town. I couldn't change the town and as an older man, I tried to change my family.

Now, as an old man, I realize the only thing I can change is myself, and suddenly I realize that if long ago I had changed myself, I could have made an impact on my family. My family and I could have made an impact on our town. Their impact could have changed the nation and I could indeed have changed the world.

Unknown Monk, A.D. 1100

ABOUT THE AUTHOR

Sal Convento, MSEL

Mr. Convento is a Two-Time World Champion. A graduate of the U.S. Naval Academy, he served in the U.S. Navy for 10.5 years as a Surface Warfare Officer and Naval Aviator. He holds a Master's of Science Degree in Executive Leadership from the University of San Diego. A practitioner of the Martial Arts for over 28 years, he earned a Fourth Degree Master Instructor in World Tang Soo Do and a Fourth Degree Black Belt in Karate Do. He is owner and Chief Instructor of U.S. Karate Academy in San Diego, California. He lives in San Diego, California with his beautiful wife, Kristin.

www.salconvento.com

A portion of the proceeds from the sale of this book will be donated to benefit Kicks For Kids, a non-profit organization founded by Sal Convento in December 2012, to help underprivileged children attain a Martial Arts education and training to the rank of Black Belt.

Made in the USA
Columbia, SC
30 September 2023

23583848R00071